INTERNATIONAL DEVELOPMENT IN FOCUS

Developing China's Ports

How the Gateways to Economic Prosperity Were Revived

BERNARD ARITUA, HEI CHIU, LU CHENG, SHEILA FARRELL, AND PETER DE LANGEN

WORLD BANK GROUP

Contents

Foreword   *vii*
Acknowledgments   *ix*
About the Authors   *xi*
Executive Summary   *xiii*
Abbreviations   *xxi*

CHAPTER 1 **The Growth of China's Port Sector**   **1**

Introduction   1
Rapid economic growth and the port sector in China   1
Growing port productivity and connectivity   7
The emergence of strong Chinese port and shipping companies   11
Ports and special economic zones   13
The expansion of port-hinterland networks   13
Dry ports   14
Note   16
References   17

CHAPTER 2 **Reforming and Developing China's Port Sector**   **19**

Introduction   19
China's approach to macroeconomic development   19
Regional economic development policies and their impact on
    the port sector   22
Port governance and reform   26
Diversifying the financing of port infrastructure   31
Planning and development of ports and port cities   40
Hinterland transport policies and connectivity   48
Environmental policies for ports   61
Upgrading skills and digital technology capabilities in ports   63
Notes   72
References   72

CHAPTER 3 **Lessons from China's Port Sector Development**   **79**

Introduction   79
Macroeconomic and regional development: A holistic approach   79
Port-hinterland connectivity and port cities   82
Human resources and innovation   84
Port governance and finance   85
References   90

Appendix A **Policies Affecting Multimodal Transport in China, 2011–19** **91**

Appendix B **Complete List of China's Dry Ports** **93**

Boxes

1.1   The long history of ports in China   8
1.2   The distinction between coastal and river ports and the major role of river ports in China   9
1.3   Yiwu dry port and the evolution of small-merchandise export inspection   15
2.1   Port development under China's 11th, 12th, 13th, and 14th Five-Year Plans   23
2.2   Port consolidation: The Shanghai International Port Group and its "Yangtze Strategy"   32
2.3   The World Bank's first loans to Guangzhou, Shanghai, and Tianjin   33
2.4   Port construction fees   37
2.5   Ports as an anchor for growth: The case of the Binhai New Area   42
2.6   A model for the development of port cities: The case of Shenzhen   43
2.7   Complexity in port development beyond the city border: The case of Shanghai   44
2.8   Joint ventures linked to ports: The success of Daqin Railways   51
2.9   Cooperation between the Ports of Dalian and Shenyang   58
2.10   The Port of Ningbo-Zhoushan   59
2.11   Two examples of digitalization initiatives from the ports of Xiamen and Shanghai   68
2.12   Current goals of information and communication technology development in China's ports   70
3.1   Lesson 1: Port development should not stop at the port gate   80
3.2   Lesson 2: Consider how to balance decentralization, central coordination, and local initiative   82
3.3   Lesson 3: Long-term competitiveness depends on strong networks and corridors linking ports with hinterlands   83
3.4   Lesson 4: Deploy land-use strategies to maximize the economic benefits of ports   83
3.5   Lesson 5: Invest in human capital and innovation as drivers of productivity and efficiency   84
3.6   Lesson 6: Government plays a role in creating the right environment for port financing while balancing economic, social, and environmental objectives   86
3.7   Lesson 7: Broaden access to the finance and public support needed to develop a competitive port ecosystem   87
3.8   Lesson 8: Test the waters before scaling up   88

Figures

1.1   China's GDP per capita and as a percentage of world GDP, 1978–2019   2
1.2   China's international merchandise trade, 1978–2019   2
1.3   Value of China's exports as a share of world exports, 1978–2019   3
1.4   Throughput of major coastal ports in China and selected global comparators, 2019   5
1.5   Length of vessel time in China's ports and average payload, 1985–2018   6
1.6   Growth of coastal and river ports in China, 1978–2020   8
B1.2.1 Throughput of coastal ports and river ports in China, 1978–2020   9
1.7   Container volumes of China's coastal ports, 1978–2018   10
1.8   Composition of cargo handled in China's major coastal ports, 1978 and 2018   10
1.9   Composition of China's seaborne trade, 2018   10
1.10   Change in liner shipping connectivity index for China, 2004–19   11

1.11   Length of transport routes of roads, inland waterways, and
       railways in China, 1978–2018   14
2.1   China's port governance model, 1978–83   28
2.2   China's port governance model, 1984–91   29
2.3   China's port governance model, 2001–11   30
2.4   Investment levels in China's port sector, 1978–2020   34
2.5   Evolution of financing sources for China's port sector, 1978–2020   34
2.6   Funding sources for investments in port infrastructure and facilities   35
2.7   Illustration of revenue sources for port enterprises   36
2.8   Potential forms of entry for foreign companies in China's port sector   39
2.9   Foreign direct investment in China's ports, 1991–2019   40
2.10   Relationship between population size and port throughput in
       several Chinese port cities   41
2.11   Relationship between port throughput and GDP in several Chinese port
       cities, 1980–2015   41
2.12   Volume of freight moved by roads, inland waterways, and railways
       in China, 1978–2018   48
2.13   Investments in inland waterways and volumes handled at inland ports
       in China, 1978–2018   54
2.14   Chinese freight traffic, by mode of transport, 1978–2018   55
2.15   Basic functions of inland dry ports   57
B2.10.1 Growth of intermodal sea-rail container shipments at the Port of
       Ningbo-Zhoushan, 2012–18   60
2.16   Proportion of operational and technical workers, and of staff with
       bachelor's degree and higher at specific ports, 2018   65

Maps

1.1   China's coastal ports   4
1.2   China's top river ports, 2018   5
1.3   China's inland dry ports, 2019   6
2.1   The first generation of special economic zones in China, 1980–92   24
2.2   Spatial pattern of China's urbanization based on "clusters along the
       axes"   26
2.3   Integration of port groups   31
B2.7.1 The relocation of the Port of Shanghai to Zhanghuabang, Waigaoqiao, and
       Yangshan   45
B2.8.1 Daqin line linking Datong to Qinhuangdao Port   51
2.4   The 2-1-2-18 Inland Waterway Network in China   53
2.5   Ship emission control zone regions in China   63

Photos

2.1   Qingdao city and port   46
2.2   Rail-port connectivity, Qinhuangdao Port   47
2.3   Bulk terminal, Port of Yantai   50
2.4   Wind power, Port of Wuxi   62
B2.11.1 Inland container barges operating at the automated container
       terminal at Yangshan, Port of Shanghai   69

Tables

1.1   World's 10 busiest ports, by cargo throughput, 2019   3
1.2   World's top 10 container ports, by container throughput, 2019   4
1.3   Ranking of top 10 container ports in China, the United States, and
       Europe, by twenty-foot equivalent units and container port
       performance index, 2020   7
1.4   Turnover of listed Chinese port enterprises, 2018–20   12
1.5   World rankings of port operators, 1996–2019   12
1.6   SEZs in China's largest container ports   13
1.7   Cargo volumes on China's main waterways, 2017   14

1.8   Top 10 ports in China, by container volume moved by rail-sea transport, 2018   16

2.1   Phases in China's port development and key reforms during those phases, 1978–present   20

2.2   Major policy initiatives, 1978–present   20

B2.2.1   Investments by SIPG in port and terminal companies   32

2.3   Length of national and joint-venture railways in China, 1995 and 2013   51

B2.10.1 Selected rail service routes from the Port of Ningbo-Zhoushan, 2018   59

2.4   Customs clearance measures enacted by the General Administration of Customs, 2006, 2014, and 2017   60

2.5   Information and communication technology systems in major ports of China   71

A.1   Policies concerning multimodal transport in China, 2011–19   91

B.1   Profile of China's dry ports   94

Foreword

China celebrated the 40th anniversary of its "reform and opening up" in 2018. This period of rapid economic growth and poverty reduction began in 1978. More than 800 million people—equivalent to about 75 percent of the population of Africa—have been lifted out of poverty, and China progressed from being one of the poorest nations to becoming an upper-middle-income country. China's share of global gross domestic product (GDP) increased from 1.8 percent in 1980 to about 18 percent in 2021, and national GDP expanded 25-fold, exceeding all expectations and targets. The details of how this outstanding development outcome was achieved are evolving. Overall, however, the reforms that led to this dramatic growth included experimentation in policy and institutional design along with the gradual opening of the economy to market forces, foreign direct investment, and targeted initiatives. As the backbone for the drivers of growth, the transport sector forms an important part of China's growth story. During the period of rapid growth, China also developed the transport system and infrastructure at a speed and scale that are unmatched. From 1990 to 2021, China added more than 120,000 kilometers of railways, 130,000 kilometers of expressways, 3 million kilometers of roads, and 125,000 kilometers of navigable inland waterway transportation.

Gateway ports were especially important in China's economic transformation, which started with the development of the coastal regions. In 1984, 14 coastal cities started opening to foreign direct investments, with gateway ports serving as the fulcrum for coastal economies. As a result, these cities enjoyed significant economic growth. For example, Shanghai's GDP per capita increased from ¥ 3,232 in 1984 to ¥ 173,800 in 2021. Additionally, China's investments in the coastal regions radiated out from the three major port groupings—the Yangtze River Delta in the center, the Pearl River Delta in the south, and the Bohai Rim in the north toward the interior hinterland. By 2021, China was home to seven of the world's top ten busiest ports. Along with other smaller ports on the coastline and inland ports, the port system was crucial to overall national economic growth and spreading the benefits of prosperity.

The World Bank has been a partner with China on this journey of economic and social transformation. The first World Bank transport sector loan and technical assistance to China in 1982 was to the ports of Guangzhou, Shanghai, and Tianjin because these three ports were considered critical for the growth path of

China. In the past three decades, the World Bank has approved more than 110 transportation projects in China, with a total investment of $19 billion. The World Bank and China's Ministry of Transport have jointly developed the Transport Transformation and Innovation Knowledge Platform (TransFORM) program—a flagship knowledge platform positioned to share Chinese and international transport experiences and facilitate learning and knowledge exchange between China and World Bank client countries. What can other countries learn from China's success? Chinese practices and experiences are relevant for emerging economies looking for sustainable solutions to transport development challenges. Through TransFORM, the World Bank is analyzing China's experience in five areas of transport—high-speed rail, highways, urban transport, ports, and inland waterways—to identify lessons that are transferrable from China to other emerging economies. The first report was on high-speed rail development, followed by a report on inland waterway transport. This report examines the port sector and covers a range of why, what, and how questions.

Despite strong interest from various emerging economies to learn from China's experiences on how to accelerate economic benefits through strategic transport infrastructure development, the relevant information is not readily available in an accessible format. What China achieved is remarkable and extremely informative; however, "how" and "why" is especially relevant and provides valuable lessons for other countries. Of course, not all the experiences and lessons are directly applicable to every country; this report, however, provides the first in-depth record that other countries can draw on in making informed decisions.

Martin Raiser
Country Director
China, Mongolia, and the Republic of Korea
The World Bank

Fei Weijun
President
China Waterborne Transport Research Institute
China

Vivien Foster
Chief Economist
Infrastructure Practice Group
The World Bank

Acknowledgments

This report is an output of the Transport Global Practice of the World Bank Group. It was prepared by a team led by Bernard Aritua (senior infrastructure specialist, World Bank), Hei Chiu (transport specialist, World Bank), and Lu Cheng (senior researcher, China Waterborne Transport Research Institute [WTI]). The report was part of wider research on Gateway Ports Development for Economic Transformation. The research was initiated by Hua Tan (senior transport specialist, World Bank) and benefited immensely from the technical guidance of Sheila Farrell (consultant), who has extensive experience in the port sector in emerging economies. Technical guidance and writing of the report also benefited from the assistance of Robin C. Carruthers (consultant and former lead transport economist, World Bank), Esther Chiew (senior data scientist, Sandia National Laboratories), Peter de Langen (principal consultant, Ports & Logistics Advisory, and part-time professor, Copenhagen Business School), Richard van Liere (inland waterways transportation expert, STC Nestra), and James Jixian Wang (professor, University of Hong Kong).

The content draws on primary research carried out by WTI. The following researchers from WTI carried out the primary research: Wu Jialu, Zhang Zhehui, Wang Bin, Yu Xiujuan, Ning Tao, Zhang Yongming, Xing Husong, Peng Chuansheng, Li Xinyi, Chen Yihao, Tang Zhenyu, Guo Yanchen, Ma Yanyan, Sun Ting, Cai Ouchen, and Yang Yahe. The researchers thank Dr. Jia Dashan, vice president of WTI, for guidance and oversight of the research. Tong Mengda from the Port of Ningbo-Zhoushan and Chen Guoping from the Port of Zhenjiang contributed to the operational aspects of the research. A team from PricewaterhouseCoopers (PwC), including Hongbin Jiang, Yawen Hou, Shu Zhang and others, carried out analysis and research on issues related to port financing and reforms in China. Professor Qin Yu from the National University of Singapore carried out economic modeling and analysis of the impacts of China's ports and hinterlands, supported by Zhang Jialiang from Peking University. This rigorous research underpins the empirical evidence on the economic impact of ports.

The team acknowledges the excellent discussions with and feedback from various policy makers and officials from public organizations responsible for inland waterway transportation and ports in various countries. The authors are grateful to experts from the following organizations for sharing their experience and insights and for providing data: Indian Ports Association, Inland Waterways Authority of India, Kenya Ports Authority, Ningbo Transportation Committee, Port Management Association of West and Central Africa, Port of Antwerp International, Port of Beira, Port of Djibouti, Port of Los Angeles, Port of Ningbo-Zhoushan, Port of Rotterdam, Port of Shanghai, Shanghai Transportation Committee, Tanzania Ports Authority, and Transnet National Ports Authority.

Invaluable expert advice was received from the following peer reviewers: Ninan Oommen Biju, Chen Jihong, Gopal Krishna, Yinyin Lam, and Andrew Losos. The report also benefited from reviews and improvements offered by Damon Luciano, Zijing Niu, Lingxiao Ran, and Xiang Xu. The authors are grateful to Martin Raiser (country director, China, Mongolia, and the Republic of Korea, World Bank) and Benedictus Eijbergen and Binyam Reja (managers, Transport Global Practice, World Bank) for their guidance and support in preparing this report, and to Vivien Foster (chief economist, Infrastructure Practice Group, World Bank) for her technical review.

The authors also wish to acknowledge various reports and policy documents that have been referred to in the study and referenced in this report.

The authors are grateful to Sara Sultan (senior knowledge management officer, World Bank) and Jung Eun Oh (Infrastructure program leader, China and Mongolia, World Bank) for advice on publishing and dissemination of the report. Steven Kennedy provided editorial support, and Azeb Afework and Yumeng Zhu provided outstanding operational and administrative support.

Funding for this report was provided by the China–World Bank Group Partnership Facility (CWPF). The objective of CWPF is to assist member countries of the participating World Bank Group organizations in achieving inclusive and sustainable development. This report is disseminated under the umbrella of TransFORM, the Transport Transformation and Innovation Knowledge Platform, which is jointly convened by the government of China and the World Bank.

About the Authors

Bernard Aritua is a senior infrastructure specialist at the World Bank. He has worked in the field of infrastructure development and economic policy for more than 20 years. During this time, he has led and provided technical input on policy analysis, regulation, institutional reform, and the technical design of major highways, railways, inland waterways transportation, freight logistics, and multimodal transport. He has published more than 50 reports, as well as articles in peer-reviewed international journals, and has contributed to several international conferences. Before joining the World Bank, he worked in both the private and public sectors. He has lived and worked in several countries and regions, including Germany, the United Kingdom, Africa, Eastern Europe, the Middle East, and, more recently, China and India. He is a member of the Chartered Institution of Highways and Transportation and the Institute of Asset Management and is a Chartered Engineer. He holds a PhD in civil engineering from the University of Leeds.

Lu Cheng is a senior researcher at the China Waterborne Transport Research Institute (WTI). He has more than 20 years of experience in the waterway transport industry and is a respected specialist on inland waterway transport, intermodal, port management, and logistics. He has led and been involved in many key national and ministerial projects in China's waterway transport industry, focusing on market analysis, policy design, planning, knowledge exchange, and training. He has abundant consulting experience for government, public agencies, and private enterprises in China. He is actively involved in research and consulting in waterways transportation and logistics sectors for international institutions. To support development of sustainable transport, he is currently providing support for the APEC Port Services Network and has gained considerable experience on knowledge exchange, capacity building, and sustainability promotion programs such as the Green Port Award System. Cheng holds a master's degree in transport economy from Shanghai Maritime University.

Hei Chiu is a transport specialist at the World Bank. She works on various lending and technical advisory projects in the Middle East and North Africa, South Asia, and China, including regional railway connectivity, urban transport, decarbonizing transport, and innovative pilot programs. She holds a bachelor's degree in civil engineering from Tsinghua University, and a master's degree in engineering and a PhD in transportation planning from the University of Tokyo.

Peter de Langen is the owner and principal consultant of Ports & Logistics Advisory (PLA), which he founded in 2013, and is a part-time professor at Copenhagen Business School. PLA aims to provide high-impact contributions to projects and organizations and is active in boardroom advisory, research, and executive education in ports and logistics worldwide. PLA works for leading companies and governments in the ports industry including the Asian Development Bank, European Seaports Organisation, Panama Canal Authority, Port of Barcelona, Port of Rotterdam, United Nations, and the World Bank. From 2007 to 2013, he was a senior adviser in corporate strategy at the Port of Rotterdam Authority. De Langen is codirector of the knowledge dissemination platform www.porteconomics.eu, and he develops training events and regularly speaks at industry conferences. He has authored more than 50 peer-reviewed articles as well as the book *Towards a Better Ports Industry*. De Langen holds a PhD in economics from Erasmus University Rotterdam.

Sheila Farrell is a freelance consultant, specializing in port economics and finance, who undertakes project appraisal work for the main international lending agencies. She has been involved in more than 150 port projects in 65 countries, including China. Her main areas of work are business planning, investment appraisal, port reform and privatization, financial restructuring, and port tariffs. She began her career in a port engineering company, followed by 14 years at Coopers & Lybrand. Since 1992 she has had her own specialist consulting firm. She is also a visiting professor in port operations research at Imperial College London and a member of the editorial advisory board of the journal *Maritime Policy & Management*. She has written two books on the role of the private sector in financing transport infrastructure and has published many academic articles on port reform policies. Farrell holds a BSc in economics from the London School of Economics and a PhD in maritime economics from the University of Liverpool.

Executive Summary

INTRODUCTION

This report traces the development of China's port sector over the past four decades. It summarizes key policy decisions, describes the context in which they were made, and explains their impact on port and logistics development in China and on China's economic development more broadly. The report tells this story by exploring four topics through four periods. The first topic addresses the links between China's macroeconomic and regional development strategies and the development of the port sector. The second is more specific to the ports themselves and analyzes changes in port governance, including the way in which essential investments were determined and financed. The relationship of ports to the cities where they are located and to the hinterlands on which they depend is the third topic. The fourth addresses how human resource and policies in the port sector have responded to changing demands. The four periods represent the four phases of reform since 1980, each characterized by a different and evolving context that shaped policy approaches to the port sector.

The topics covered in this report were developed based on interactions with public officials involved in the port sector in several emerging economies. They are also the primary audience for the analysis presented here. However, it should be emphasized that when drawing lessons from China's experience, context matters. Few countries rival China in territorial expanse or length of coastline, both of which encourage a significant degree of domestic interport competition, stimulating reform and investment at the local level and in port governance. Few countries can match China's prolonged periods of growth, which have stimulated demand for port capacity. Finally, China's administrative model is unique. For all these reasons, the present report is intended not as a blueprint for others but rather as a contribution to the exchange of development experience.

The significance of China's changing macroeconomic context for the development of the port sector is best appreciated by dividing the past four decades into four distinct subperiods. Each of these subperiods presented different needs and opportunities for water-based transportation and generated different policy responses. One of the emerging characteristics of port development in China is its adaptability and the ability of policy makers to change course when circumstances require it.

FOUR PERIODS OF ECONOMIC GROWTH

Before China's economic opening, which began in 1978, China had a relatively small and closed economy. Per capita gross domestic product (GDP) was 5 percent of the world average, and international trade (merchandise imports and exports) accounted for only 14 percent of GDP, less than half of the world average. The State Planning Commission controlled the importation and exportation of goods, and most trading occurred through firms owned and controlled by the Ministry of Foreign Trade. China's economic opening coincided with a sharp fall in the global costs of maritime transport that resulted from the advent of containerization and increases in vessel size. This fall—along with trade liberalization and improvements in international communications—led to the globalization of manufacturing and the long period of sustained growth in international trade, of which China has been one of the principal instigators and beneficiaries. Since 1978, China's trade has grown almost continuously. By 2019, merchandise trade in China had increased to 31 percent of GDP, and that growth was a major contributor to the rise in China's per capita GDP from 5 percent of the world average in 1978 to 74 percent in 2021 (in constant 2010 US$). China's share of global exports increased from less than 2 percent in 1990 to almost 11 percent by 2018. Ports were pivotal to this growth.

Period 1: Decentralizing port management, 1978–91

During the initial period of China's economic opening, from 1978 until about 1991, China began decentralizing port management to facilitate development of special economic zones (SEZs). This period was characterized by the first steps toward reform, the opening up of the planned economy, and the use of exports as the engine of economic growth. The creation of four SEZs in 1980 to attract foreign direct investment in manufacturing was the central macroeconomic policy driving China's economic opening. Each zone was anchored on a maritime port in a coastal province.

In 1984, China began decentralizing port governance by piloting a dual-management principle of port governance at the Port of Tianjin, where both the central and municipal governments played a role. By 1989, most major ports were managed under this dual model. Provincial and city governments allocated land and provided tax advantages to stimulate port development. This period was characterized by initial steps toward the commercialization of port activities, such as allowing cargo owners to build their own facilities and permitting some foreign companies to operate container terminals, albeit under a tight regulatory framework.

Period 2: Building on the positive experiences of economic opening, 1992–2001

From 1992 through 2001, China built on the positive experiences of the initial economic opening. Following Deng Xiaoping's famous Southern Tour in 1992, economic and social reforms began to gain momentum and coalesce around a comprehensive plan to build a market-driven economy. A new policy of decentralization gave local governments more authority to approve investments and to decide how their own fiscal resources should be used.

Decentralization allowed local governments to invest in port development. In the process, local governments actively sought new sources of financing, including loans from state-owned banks and financing through capital markets. Human capital reforms—ranging from incentives-based pay for the workforce to upgraded port education and training institutions—contributed to rapid improvement in managerial and operational efficiency. Moreover, major ports started developing their own information systems to optimize efficiency. The growth center shifted northward along the coastline, and with reforms the old industrial centers such as Shanghai and surrounding areas saw a revival.

Despite rapid progress, the port industry was not developing at the pace the central government believed was needed to keep up with global economic trends and ambitions for China's role in global trade. As a result, by the late 1990s, port development received new attention, moving to the top of the central government's agenda in successive five-year plans.

Period 3: Joining the World Trade Organization and developing the "Go West" policy, 2002–11

The third period of China's port development (2002–11) coincided with joining the World Trade Organization in November 2001 and the development of the "Go West" policy. These changes marked another inflection point in the move toward a market-oriented economy requiring changes to management of the port sector. Domestic and international investment resulted in many new export-oriented processing factories. The accompanying boost in trade necessitated a further expansion of port capacity. To stimulate additional investment, the Port Law of 2004 further decentralized port governance and limited government intervention in operations and management by dividing port authorities into regulatory and commercial entities. This separation provided a stronger incentive for ports to improve their operational efficiency and competitiveness. It also encouraged joint-venture schemes, which previously had been limited, by providing legal protection and removing barriers to entry for domestic and foreign companies.

The Go West policy, introduced in 2000, was aimed explicitly at boosting the economic development of 12 western provincial-level regions—Chongqing, Sichuan, Guizhou, Yunnan, Tibet, Shanxi, Gansu, Ningxia, Xinjiang, Inner Mongolia, Guangxi, and Qinghai—that are home to more than 400 million people. With prosperity from the export-led economy concentrated up to then in the coastal regions, these western regions began to receive increasing support for infrastructure, environmental protection, education, and the development and retention of talent. From 2000 to 2016, the Chinese government invested ¥ 6.35 trillion (US$914 billion) in 300 major projects in the western regions, most of them involving infrastructure and energy. Rapidly expanding networks of roads and inland waterways, river ports, and dry ports linked the coast with the inner western regions.

As port capacity expanded, it became clear that several parts of the sector required streamlining. For example, local port enterprises' ambitious growth objectives generated excess capacity in some market segments. In response, the central government urged ports to merge into provincial port groups and to increase coordination and cooperation. Road, rail, and inland waterway corridors needed further improvement. Initially, road transport took the lead.

China's first dry port came into operation in 2002 with the aim of improving trade connectivity and lowering logistics costs. By 2008, locations for 28 dry ports had been selected; these dry ports were developed over the next decade and now total more than 70. The focus shifted from the expansion of capacity to the quality, efficiency, and sustainability of port services. Rail and inland waterways began to rival roads as options for connecting with an expanding domestic hinterland.

Period 4: Shifting the economic model, 2011–present

From 2011 onward, China began to shift its economic model toward greater reliance on innovation, services, and the development of domestic demand. China's economic planners sought to reduce dependence on resource- and energy-intensive growth and to better manage climate and environmental impacts.

As part of the transition to a less resource-dependent and more regionally balanced economy, China launched a national program in 2018 to develop 19 city clusters and metropolitan regions. The aim was to promote agglomeration, with small cities and towns integrated into urban clusters. In the short term, this program redirected growth back to coastal regions. The first three metropolitan regions taking shape are the Pearl River Delta (Guangzhou and Shenzhen), the Yangtze River Delta (based on Shanghai), and Beijing and Tianjin.

The development of emerging technologies such as the Internet of Things, big data, and artificial intelligence has been given high priority. Several initiatives related to intelligent shipping and smart ports are reorienting the entire port sector. China has adopted major "green port" technologies and management measures, including evaluation criteria to guide and regulate environmental standards, new emission-control areas, incentives for developing shore power facilities (along with regulations to promote their use), and a switch from diesel-based terminal operations to electric-powered cranes and other terminal equipment.

Although road transport remains the dominant form of surface transportation, alternative modes of transport, chiefly rail and inland waterways, have received greater attention as options for improving domestic connectivity. Looking beyond the mainland, undertakings such as the Belt and Road Initiative offer Chinese port enterprises the opportunity to continue their expansion in international partner economies.

As is the case in other countries endowed with coastlines, port expansion has had a significant impact on the economies of the cities where the ports are located. After their ports expand, fixed asset investment and foreign direct investment perform better in port cities than in neighboring cities without ports. GDP per capita also performs better in large port cities. These increased levels of economic activity can be expected to lead to greater and more secure employment and to more spatial concentration of economic activity, both of which are major benefits attributable to port development. Of course, as is the case with port cities globally, the negative impacts of ports have also been felt in gateway ports across China in the form of increased traffic, noise pollution, dust, and increases in the cost of land. Steps are being taken across China to mitigate some of these effects and to encourage the relocation of some port functions to inland locations.

LESSONS LEARNED FROM CHINA'S PORT EXPANSION

The context in which China's ports developed is unique in many ways. The surge of trade following the initial reform and opening of the economy generated demand for port capacity that most developing countries are unlikely to replicate, which made investments less risky. China's size and highly decentralized administrative system allowed for competition and a process of trial and error that would be impossible in countries with only one dominant maritime port. China's public administration has high capacity for credible policy commitments, effective coordination of private and public stakeholders, and the ability to adopt a long-term planning horizon, characteristics that are in short supply in many other countries. For all these reasons, the lessons learned from China's port expansion must not be taken as a blueprint. Nevertheless, they provide pointers for policy makers in other countries to draw on in developing their own port expansion strategies.

Macroeconomic development

Port development should not stop at the port gate. In most developing countries, the development of ports is entrusted to a single entity at arm's length from government ministries that focuses on the maritime side of ports and on their development up to the port gates. Critical links are often neglected, and ports are less profitable and economically valuable as a result. Holistic port development should consider the macroeconomic context, including logistics, trade, and transport. Connectivity between ports and their surrounding cities and regions via multimodal transport networks is particularly important.

Efficient port development requires finding the right balance between central coordination and local initiative. Before 1978, China's port sector was heavily centralized. Port ownership and governance were under the control of the Ministry of Transport (MoT), which had regulatory, administrative, and operational responsibility for ports. Local governments had no control, and all revenues from port operations accrued to the central government. Decentralization of regulatory functions to local governments, and the introduction of commercial management practices for port operations, accelerated port development but eventually resulted in overcapacity and required the establishment of regional port clusters to better align supply and demand. Only by trial and error did China find the right balance between macroeconomic planning of port investments and decentralized management to create performance incentives. Smaller countries with only one or two major ports to develop may not have that opportunity; they will need to get the right balance from the start, using evidence-based planning that goes beyond the overly optimistic projections of traffic volumes that often characterize decisions in developing countries.

Port cities and hinterlands

Long-term port competitiveness relies on good multimodal connectivity with the hinterland. Initially, China developed individual transport modes separately and therefore relied heavily on the rapidly expanding interprovincial highway network to connect cities and the hinterland. As the Go West strategy gained momentum, railways and inland waterways came to play a more prominent role.

It was thus only later that the advantages of a more integrated transport network were fully appreciated, and China is now retrofitting (at additional cost) for multimodal integration. This process has led to the creation of large logistics and manufacturing clusters in the hinterland, with reliable and competitively priced intermodal services to ports. The lesson for developing countries is that while mobilizing funds for complementary investments in rail and inland waterway networks may initially be challenging, these networks lay the foundation for long-term port competitiveness and growth. A multimodal approach should therefore be embedded in plans for port-hinterland connectivity.

Land-use strategies should maximize the economic benefits of ports. Consideration should be given to relocating port facilities so as to build a stronger port-economy ecosystem. Many of China's major ports have moved to new locations. In some cases, the new areas were partly funded by revenues derived from conversion of the original location to higher-value commercial and residential use. Local governments have transformed some port cities in accordance with long-term plans for the areas surrounding new port sites and investments in infrastructure for port-related industries and their workers. This approach has allowed economic development objectives to be balanced with the growing demand for livable urban spaces as China's coastal cities have grown wealthier. The experience shows that, in large agglomerations, relocating port activities to areas with room for expansion of port, logistics, and manufacturing activities can facilitate the regeneration of city centers. China's land-use planning institutions and land-based financing models have greatly facilitated this transformation.

Human resources and innovation

Human capital development and innovation can be powerful drivers of port productivity and efficiency. China has used effective workforce planning to create a culture of responsibility and accountability within its ports. Rapid technological changes in port operations have made port workers an increasingly valuable resource, requiring continued investment in their training and career development. Investments in human resources are highly cost-effective but too often neglected or hampered by vested interests. Chinese port operators have developed strong management systems featuring specialist training, performance-related pay, and good channels of communication. These lessons could be quite widely applicable.

Innovation in information technology became another driver of efficiency in Chinese ports. New technology is producing large efficiency gains by coordinating the actions of many different players in port supply chains and allowing each worker to accomplish more. Although Chinese ports initially used software obtained from international sources, most now develop their own. Technology sharing between ports and supply chain partners has emerged to some degree and has been incorporated into the software development process. Customs services have played a large role in this reform, helping China significantly reduce trade costs and thus stimulate port competitiveness.

Port governance and finance

In China's context, state ownership of port enterprises has facilitated coordination with broader development objectives while allowing for a strong commercial orientation. State ownership of port enterprises in China ensured that all actions and investments not only supported port development strategies within and beyond the port gate, but also were consistent with broad macro-economic and social policies. Such coordination need not depend on who owns and operates port assets, but in an environment of relatively weak legal and contract-management institutions, coordination within the state sector was arguably easier than it would have been under a public-private partnership. State-owned ports also benefited from implicit government guarantees in raising funding and thus financing their rapid expansion at relatively low cost. Strong human resource and management practices ensured that port enterprises, despite being state owned, remained performance oriented and had incentives to adopt new technologies and business practices, turning them into globally competitive port operators. In this context, China's experience may not be easy to replicate. Few other countries can use competition between local governments and state-owned enterprises (SOEs) as a yardstick with which to assess performance. In many countries, governance weaknesses within the public sector have turned SOEs into a source of rent-seeking, poor performance, and significant implicit or explicit fiscal risks. Without China's track record of performance-based public sector management, its state ownership model might not have done so well.

Although port operations can be commercialized quickly, public support may be needed to develop a competitive port ecosystem. China's initial reforms in the port sector aligned the incentives of local governments with port development. In addition to delegating regulatory and operational responsibilities to the local level, the MoT also allowed a share of port profits to be reinvested. The subsequent clear separation between regulatory and operational functions allowed state-owned port enterprises to focus on maximizing efficiency, while local governments frequently adjusted port charges and fees to optimize revenue generation and cost competitiveness. Local governments also sought to diversify sources of funding for port development early on by forming joint ventures to attract foreign direct investment, which also brought new technology and modern management practices. When port operations were commercialized and could attract debt finance, public support shifted to ensuring connectivity with the hinterland and developing a port city ecosystem. Tax incentives for the relocation of industries to new port areas also enhanced their economic attractiveness. State-owned banks provided funding to port enterprises throughout the port commercialization.

The rapid growth and industrialization of China's cities over the past four decades has provided a strong revenue base for public support of the port sector. However, the problems of excess capacity that arose during the 2000s show that China's approach may come with significant efficiency losses. Countries with more limited fiscal space may need to be more discriminating about where to direct public support.

Testing the waters before scaling up is important. Chinese port reforms have not been free of false starts, but there has been a willingness to change course when policies failed to produce desired results. Pilot projects play an important role in this approach to policy development. For example, in reforming the port governance model, pilot programs in the ports of Tianjin and Dalian offered different outcomes on the role of local government authorities in port development. The Tianjin model of dual management and partial decentralization was refined and adopted nationwide, whereas the Dalian model of complete decentralization was dropped, and its positive lessons were integrated into the

Tianjin model. The same approach was used for the adoption of innovations in digitalization and financing.

China's ability to reform through pilots and through trial and error derives in part from the vast size of its territory and hence the ability to create benchmark competition across multiple locations, with practices that have proven themselves locally eventually being adopted nationwide. Few other countries are as large and decentralized as China. However, China's pragmatic approach to formulating policy, evaluating outcomes, and being willing to change course may well have broader applicability.

THE RELEVANCE OF CHINA'S EXPERIENCE

China's ports and related supply chains are among the most efficient and well-connected in the world. The institutional arrangements for port management have facilitated ports' integration into international supply chains and enabled high levels of connectivity with China's hinterlands. After a relatively slow start, China's ports now take advantage of the latest developments in digital technology and appear to have the capacity to absorb future digitalization.

Achieving these outcomes was not easy and did not follow a linear path; much is still left to be done. Strategies and policies have changed over time in response to what has worked and what has not, and to a changing external environment. Strategies and policies are still evolving to meet new challenges and to take advantage of new technologies.

As discussed above, China's context differs significantly from that of most developing countries. Thus, this report does not provide a toolkit or blueprint for port sector reform and development. Some broad conclusions can be drawn, however, among them (1) the importance of integrating port development with national development strategies; (2) the critical links between ports, port cities, and the hinterland in determining the economic value of port development and the financial viability of port investments; (3) the importance of strong management and human resource practices in ensuring efficient port operations and supporting technological upgrades; and (4) the advisability of taking a commercial approach to port development, operation, and financing, ideally enhanced by complementary public investments to develop surrounding infrastructure and a port ecosystem. China has opted for state ownership of its major ports and mobilized significant public funding, supported by a strong, performance-based public management system and the judicious use of competition among localities to drive port expansion. These aspects of China's model may be difficult to emulate, in part because they have generated efficiency losses through excess capacity that countries with more limited domestic sources of financing may not be able to afford.

Abbreviations

BCE	before the Common Era
CE	Common Era
CMG	China Merchants Group
CMSK	China Merchants Shekou Industrial Zone Holdings
COSCO	China Ocean Shipping Co.
COVID-19	coronavirus disease
CPPI	container port performance index
dwt	deadweight tonnage
ETDZ	economic and technological development zone
GDP	gross domestic product
ICT	information and communication technology
LSCI	liner shipping connectivity index
MoT	Ministry of Transport
SAR	special administrative region
SEZ	special economic zone
SIPG	Shanghai International Port Group
SOE	state-owned enterprise
TEU	twenty-foot equivalent unit
WTI	China Waterborne Transport Research Institute
¥	Chinese yuan
US$	US dollars

1 The Growth of China's Port Sector

INTRODUCTION

This chapter provides an overview of China's port sector, including its size, structure, and evolution over the past 40 years. It also describes the relationship between the rapid growth of China's economy and international trade and the growth of Chinese ports. It discusses the development of special economic zones in proximity to ports. The chapter concludes with a brief description of the emergence, growth, and internationalization of Chinese port companies and the evolution of networks connecting ports with the hinterlands.

RAPID ECONOMIC GROWTH AND THE PORT SECTOR IN CHINA

The role of transport investment in generating and spreading economic benefits is well known, and China's port sector has played a large part in transforming the country's economy by integrating it with the rest of the world. Over the past 40 years, China has invested heavily in port development, an effort that has gone hand in hand with economic growth. In 1978, the start date of the reforms that transformed China into a socialist market economy, the country's economy was still relatively small and closed. Per capita gross domestic product (GDP) was 5 percent of the world average, and international trade (merchandise imports and exports) accounted for only 14 percent of GDP, less than half of the world average at the time. By 2018, China's per capita GDP had increased by a factor of 25 in constant prices (a compound annual growth rate of 17.6 percent), while its share of world GDP had increased from 1.7 percent in 1978 to 16.1 percent (figure 1.1). Between 1978 and 2018, China's merchandise trade increased from 14 percent to 33 percent of GDP, while globally, trade increased from 28 percent to 46 percent of world GDP.

China's entry into the World Trade Organization in 2001 was followed by a period of rapid trade-led growth. Between 2001 and 2011, the rate of growth of GDP held steady at an average of 15.3 percent a year, but the growth rate for international trade rose to 21.7 percent a year over the same period, despite the dip caused by the 2008 global recession (figure 1.2).

FIGURE 1.1

China's GDP per capita and as a percentage of world GDP, 1978–2019

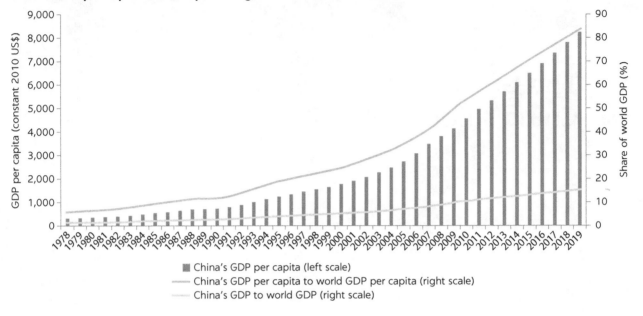

Source: World Bank.

FIGURE 1.2

China's international merchandise trade, 1978–2019

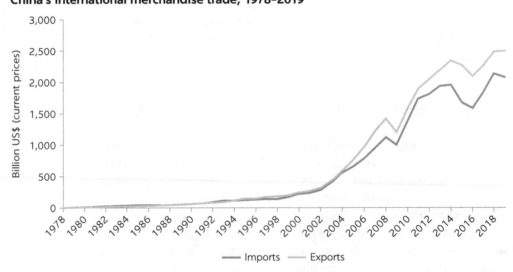

Source: World Bank.

This rapid growth was anchored in an export-led economy. In two decades, China became the world's largest manufacturer, as illustrated by the growing proportion of global exports originating from China (figure 1.3). The growth in trade led to a massive expansion of China's port facilities. Between 1985 and 2017, throughput at the country's coastal ports increased by an annual average of 11 percent, while container traffic increased even faster, at 21 percent. By 2018, the throughput of these coastal ports had increased from 198 million tons at the start of the reform period to 9.5 billion tons (Ministry of Transport, calculated by China Waterborne Transport Research Institute [WTI]).

Between 1978 and 2018, China built 2,311 new berths for vessels of more than 10,000 deadweight tonnage, mostly in the coastal ports, an average of 57 new deep-sea berths a year (Ministry of Transport 2018, 2019), equivalent to building a major new port the size of Marseille-Fos every 10 months over 40 years (Ministry of Transport, calculated by WTI). In addition, a further 630 berths were built each year for smaller ships, mostly at China's coastal and river ports. The growth in exports necessitated a dramatic expansion in port infrastructure.

As of 2019, eight of the world's ten busiest ports by cargo volume and seven of the top ten container ports were in China (tables 1.1 and 1.2).

As China grew, port infrastructure expanded rapidly to meet ballooning demand. The locations of key coastal ports are in map 1.1. By international standards many of these are now very large. As shown in figure 1.4, the throughput of most of China's ports dwarfs that of most ports around the world. This was not always the case, and how the port sector grew to handle swelling traffic holds lessons for smaller ports elsewhere. (For the locations of China's major river ports and dry ports, see maps 1.2 and 1.3, respectively.) Figure 1.5 shows how the ports have also become more efficient.

FIGURE 1.3

Value of China's exports as a share of world exports, 1978–2019

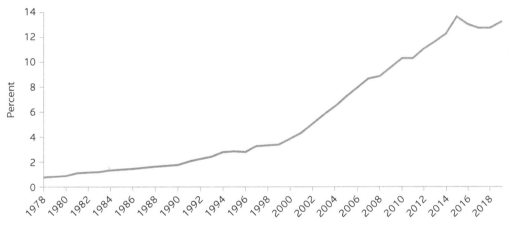

Source: United Nations Conference on Trade and Development Statistics, https://unctad.org/statistics.

TABLE 1.1 **World's 10 busiest ports, by cargo throughput, 2019**

WORLD RANKING	PORT	COUNTRY	CARGO THROUGHPUT (MILLION TONS)
1	Ningbo-Zhoushan	China	809.8
2	Shanghai	China	776.0
3	Singapore	Singapore	559.6
4	Tianjin	China	500.0
5	Guangzhou	China	455.1
6	Suzhou	China	454.3
7	Qingdao	China	450.0
8	Tangshan	China	446.2
9	Rotterdam	The Netherlands	440.5
10	Dalian	China	408.4

Source: China Shipping Database, http://www.shippingdata.cn.

TABLE 1.2 **World's top 10 container ports, by container throughput, 2019**

WORLD RANKING	PORT	COUNTRY/ECONOMY	CONTAINER THROUGHPUT (MILLION TEU)
1	Shanghai	China	43.31
2	Singapore	Singapore	37.20
3	Ningbo-Zhoushan	China	27.53
4	Shenzhen	China	25.77
5	Guangzhou	China	22.83
6	Busan	Korea, Rep.	21.91
7	Qingdao	China	21.01
8	Hong Kong SAR, China	Hong Kong SAR, China	18.36
9	Tianjin	China	17.30
10	Rotterdam	The Netherlands	14.81

Source: China Shipping Database, http://www.shippingdata.cn.
Note: TEU = twenty-foot equivalent unit.

MAP 1.1

China's coastal ports

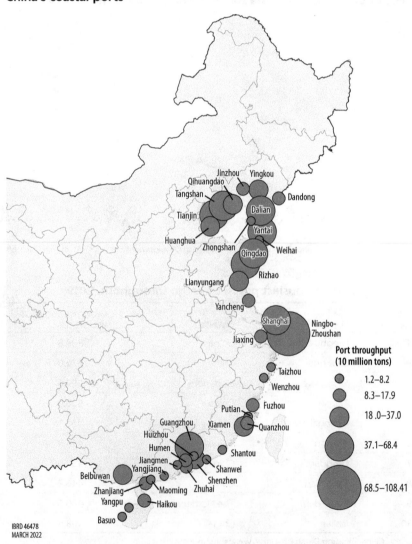

IBRD 46478
MARCH 2022

Source: World Bank, based on data from the China Waterborne Transport Research Institute (WTI).

Throughput of major coastal ports in China and selected global comparators, 2019

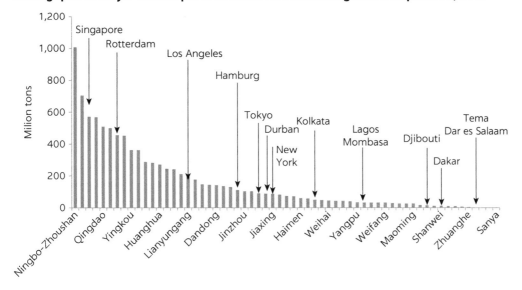

Sources: IHS Markit 2019, and National Bureau of Statistics of China 2020.

China's top river ports, 2018

Source: World Bank, based on data from the China Waterborne Transport Research Institute (WTI).
Note: dwt = deadweight tonnage.

MAP 1.3
China's inland dry ports, 2019

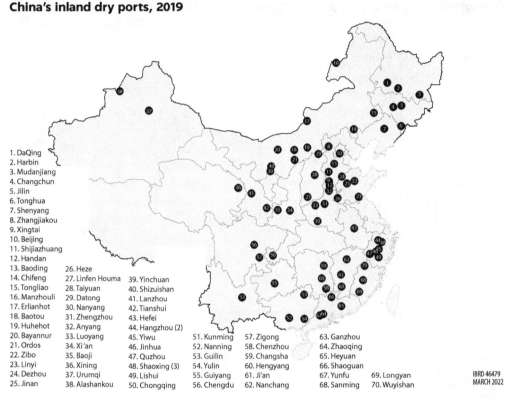

1. DaQing
2. Harbin
3. Mudanjiang
4. Changchun
5. Jilin
6. Tonghua
7. Shenyang
8. Zhangjiakou
9. Xingtai
10. Beijing
11. Shijiazhuang
12. Handan
13. Baoding
14. Chifeng
15. Tongliao
16. Manzhouli
17. Erlianhot
18. Baotou
19. Huhehot
20. Bayannur
21. Ordos
22. Zibo
23. Linyi
24. Dezhou
25. Jinan
26. Heze
27. Linfen Houma
28. Taiyuan
29. Datong
30. Nanyang
31. Zhengzhou
32. Anyang
33. Luoyang
34. Xi'an
35. Baoji
36. Xining
37. Urumqi
38. Alashankou
39. Yinchuan
40. Shizuishan
41. Lanzhou
42. Tianshui
43. Hefei
44. Hangzhou (2)
45. Yiwu
46. Jinhua
47. Quzhou
48. Shaoxing (3)
49. Lishui
50. Chongqing
51. Kunming
52. Nanning
53. Guilin
54. Yulin
55. Guiyang
56. Chengdu
57. Zigong
58. Chenzhou
59. Changsha
60. Hengyang
61. Ji'an
62. Nanchang
63. Ganzhou
64. Zhaoqing
65. Heyuan
66. Shaoguan
67. Yunfu
68. Sanming
69. Longyan
70. Wuyishan

IBRD 46479
MARCH 2022

Source: World Bank, based on data from the China Waterborne Transport Research Institute (WTI).

FIGURE 1.5
Length of vessel time in China's ports and average payload, 1985–2018

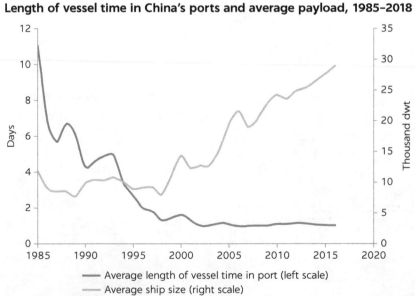

— Average length of vessel time in port (left scale)
— Average ship size (right scale)

Source: China Waterborne Transport Research Institute (WTI).
Note: DWT = deadweight tonnage.

GROWING PORT PRODUCTIVITY AND CONNECTIVITY

Since 1978, the productivity of ports in China has increased rapidly, with average tons per meter of quay at the coastal ports increasing by two-thirds between 1978 (6,365 tons per meter) and 2018 (11,076 tons per meter). The marked increase that occurred between 2005 and 2015 resulted from a combination of the following factors: containerization, increases in ship size, and improvements in cargo handling technology and port management. By 2015, productivity had risen to more than 10,000 tons per meter of quay. However, research suggests that productivity in some river ports is still below par, suggesting room for further improvement in productivity (Ye, Qi, and Xu 2020).

The extent of productivity improvements at the 14 coastal ports can be seen in the average vessel payload, which increased from 12,000 tons in 1985 to slightly less than 30,000 tons in 2018. At the same time, average ship turnround times fell from 11 days to 1 day. Table 1.3 shows that productivity in China's largest container ports compares favorably with that of the 10 largest such ports in the United States and Europe. The table ranks ports based on the elapsed time between when a ship reaches a port to its departure from the berth after completing its cargo exchange, a measure known as the container port performance index.

Box 1.1 shows that China has had a long history with ports and of taking advantage of river ports and seaports as gateways to trade.

The cargo throughput of China's ports increased 50-fold between 1978 and 2020, from 280 million tons to 14.5 billion tons, an average annual growth rate of

TABLE 1.3 Ranking of top 10 container ports in China, the United States, and Europe, by twenty-foot equivalent units and container port performance index, 2020

RANK BY TEU	CHINA		UNITED STATES		EUROPE	
	PORT	RANK BY CPPI	PORT	RANK BY CPPI	PORT	CPPI
1	Shanghai[a]	28	Los Angeles	328	Rotterdam	116
2	Ningbo-Zhoushan	20	Long Beach	333	Antwerp	86
3	Shenzhen[b]	3	New York and New Jersey	89	Hamburg	280
4	Guangzhou-Nansha	4	Savannah	279	Piraeus	93
5	Qingdao	8	Northwest Seaport Alliance (Ports of Seattle and Tacoma)	236	Valencia	283
6	Hong Kong SAR, China	7	Hampton Roads, Virginia	85	Algeciras	10
7	Tianjin	218	Houston	266	Bremerhaven	41
8	Xiamen	62	Oakland	332	Felixstowe	313
9	Dalian	33	Charleston	95	Gioia Tauro	142
10	Yingkou	—	Jacksonville	161	Barcelona	76

Source: World Bank 2021.
Note: — = not available; CPPI = container port performance index (a measure of elapsed time between when a ship reaches a port to its departure from the berth after completing its cargo exchange); TEU = twenty-foot equivalent unit.
a. The Port of Shanghai consists of three terminals: Wusongkou, Waigaoqiao, and Yangshan. Yangshan Port ranked 28th on the CPPI in 2020.
b. The Port of Shenzhen consists of facilities in Da Chan Bay, Shekou, Chiwan, Mawan, Yantian, Dongjiaotou, Fuyong, Xiadong, Shayuchong, and Neihe. Chiwan ranked third on the CPPI in 2020.

BOX 1.1

The long history of ports in China

China's first ports were developed nearly 3,000 years ago along major rivers. Chongqing, which is 2,280 kilometers inland along the Yangtze River, was one of the main inland ports at the time. The Ling Canal, built between 221 and 206 BCE, connected two major river basins—the Yangtze River and the Pearl River—thus promoting the development of inland ports in several regions. Several inland ports also developed along the Grand Canal.

During the Tang dynasty (619–907 CE), China began to trade across its traditional borders, resulting in the development of maritime ports. Foreign merchant ships from Southeast Asia, South Asia, Arabia, and East Africa frequently came to China; as a result, several seaports in southern and southeastern China flourished. During the Ming dynasty (1368–1644), Nanjing was established as China's capital, and the Port of Nanjing and other inland ports along the Yangtze River developed rapidly. After China's defeat by Britain in the First Opium War (1840–42), the country's major coastal and inland ports were opened to foreign ships, leading to rapid port growth. Shanghai emerged as China's largest port in 1853.

Since the establishment of the People's Republic of China (PRC) in 1949, the port sector has undergone various stages of development, each with unique characteristics. However, given the PRC's initial focus on domestic development, the role of ports in the economy was limited. That changed radically after 1978, with the open-door policy and the subsequent integration of China into the global economy.

FIGURE 1.6

Growth of coastal and river ports in China, 1978–2020

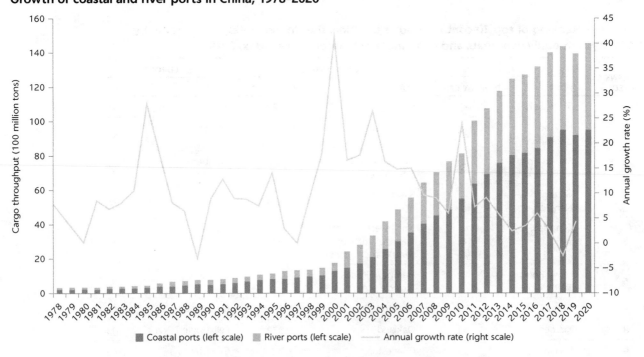

Source: China Waterborne Transport Research Institute (WTI).

10 percent (figure 1.6). This is slower than the growth in value of China's international trade (14.5 percent a year) owing to the growing importance of containerized manufactured goods. Cargo attributed to the coastal ports accounted for 9.48 billion tons in 2020 (65 percent of the total), with the remainder handled by inland river ports. See box 1.2.

BOX 1.2

The distinction between coastal and river ports and the major role of river ports in China

The *China Ports Yearbook* (China Association of Port-of-Entry 2020) provides data for 39 major coastal ports and 36 major river ports, although in practice the distinction between coastal and river ports is blurred. Many of the coastal ports are located where rivers flow into the sea and use river transport for inland distribution of at least part of their international trade. Conversely, some of the ports classified as river ports—such as Suzhou and Nantong at the entrance to the Yangtze—are developing deep-water berths and competing with coastal ports such as Shanghai for international traffic. River ports handle only half as much traffic as coastal ports, but especially during the period since 2001 their throughput has been growing faster relative to earlier periods (figure B1.2.1), in part because of China's natural geography, but also because of the failure of railways to take on the major role in container and bulk transport often seen elsewhere.

FIGURE B1.2.1

Throughput of coastal ports and river ports in China, 1978–2020

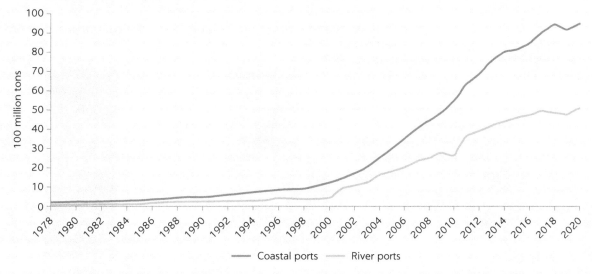

Source: China Association of Port-of-Entry 2020.

China's container throughput at coastal ports was negligible in 1978, but since 1985 it has increased at an average rate of 21 percent a year, compared with 11.2 percent a year for total coastal port throughput (figure 1.7). By 2018, it had reached 221 million twenty-foot equivalent units (TEUs).

China has 29 ports with a container throughput of more than 1 million TEU. Shanghai, with a container throughput of 43.3 million TEU in 2019, has consistently ranked as the busiest container port in the world since 2010. Whereas in 1978 bulk cargo (coal, oil, ore) made up almost 60 percent of traffic at the coastal ports, with general cargo accounting for almost all of the rest, by 2018 containers were the largest single type of cargo, accounting for almost 40 percent of the total (figure 1.8).

Chinese ports handle large volumes of coal but smaller proportions of oil and dry bulk goods than ports in other parts of the world. In 2018, containers accounted for 38 percent of Chinese ports' throughput, but only 17 percent of global seaborne trade (figure 1.9).

FIGURE 1.7
Container volumes of China's coastal ports, 1978–2018

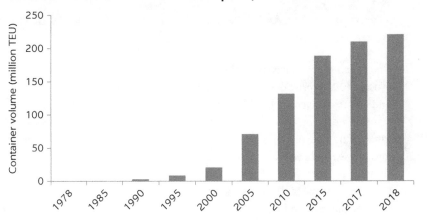

Source: Ministry of Transport.
Note: TEU = twenty-foot equivalent unit.

FIGURE 1.8
Composition of cargo handled in China's major coastal ports, 1978 and 2018

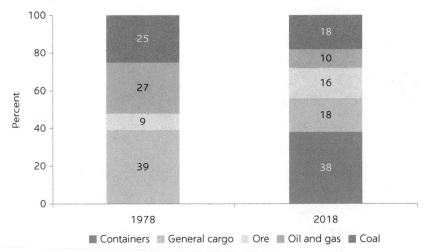

Source: China Waterborne Transport Research Institute (WTI).

FIGURE 1.9
Composition of China's seaborne trade, 2018

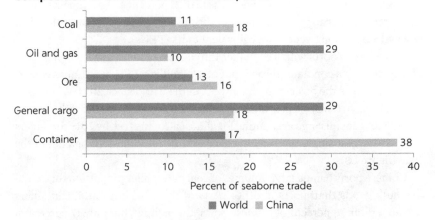

Source: UNCTAD 2020.

FIGURE 1.10
Change in liner shipping connectivity index for China, 2004–19

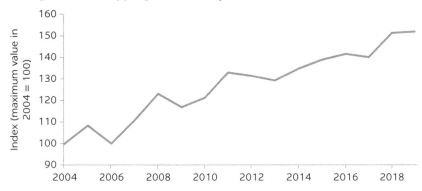

Source: UNCTADstat, https://unctadstat.unctad.org/EN/.
Note: The liner shipping connectivity index is an indicator of a country's level of integration into the maritime shipping network, and therefore into international trade. A higher index indicates greater capacity to participate in international trade.

Connectivity is an important determinant of a port's ability to participate in international trade. Every quarter, the United Nations Conference on Trade and Development publishes the liner shipping connectivity index (LSCI) as a proxy for the level of integration of countries and their ports into the maritime shipping network—and therefore into international trade. The LSCI is calculated at the country level and at the port level.[1] A higher index indicates greater capacity to participate in international trade. Figure 1.10 shows the evolution of the LSCI for China (measured by container shipping connectivity) between 2004 and 2019. Not only does China have greater port connectivity, but it is also improving its connectivity faster than its main competitors. In 2020, five of the ten most connected container ports were in China, three in other Asian countries (Republic of Korea, Malaysia, and Singapore), and the remaining two in the Hamburg–Le Havre area in Europe.

THE EMERGENCE OF STRONG CHINESE PORT AND SHIPPING COMPANIES

Over the past 40 years, Chinese port enterprises have grown into solid companies. Their turnover between 2018 and 2020 is provided in table 1.4.

The financial performance of China's ports also paved the way for increasing international activities. The most internationalized Chinese terminal company is COSCO Shipping Ports, a sister company of the Chinese Container Shipping Company, COSCO Shipping, which is the third-largest global container operator as measured by TEU throughput. In addition, China Merchants Ports has also established a substantial international presence, ranking sixth worldwide in 2019 by container throughput (measured by TEU) (table 1.5). These and other Chinese port companies have also expanded overseas, including in Belgium, Djibouti, Israel, Italy, and Malaysia.

TABLE 1.4 **Turnover of listed Chinese port enterprises, 2018–20**

	2018	2019	2020
LISTED PORT ENTERPRISE	BILLION YUAN[a]		
Shanghai International Port (Group) Co., Ltd.	38.04	36.10	26.12
Ningbo Zhoushan Port Co., Ltd.	21.88	24.32	21.27
Xiamen Port Development Co., Ltd.	13.39	14.15	15.71
Tianjin Port Co., Ltd.	13.06	12.88	13.43
Qingdao Port International Co., Ltd.	11.74	12.16	13.22
China Merchants Port Holdings Co., Ltd.	9.70	12.12	12.62
Guangzhou Port Co., Ltd.	8.64	10.42	11.25
Tangshan Port Group Co., Ltd.	10.14	11.21	7.84
Jinzhou Port Co., Ltd.	5.92	7.03	6.80
Liaoning Port Co., Ltd.	6.75	6.65	6.66
Qinhuangdao Port Co., Ltd.	6.88	6.72	6.46
Rizhao Port Co., Ltd.	5.13	5.25	5.77
Beibu Gulf Port Co., Ltd.	4.21	4.79	5.36
Chongqing Gangjiu Co., Ltd.	6.37	4.78	5.08
Zhuhai Port Shares Co., Ltd.	2.61	3.32	3.54
Jiangsu Lianyungang Port Co., Ltd.	1.32	1.42	1.62
Nanjing Port Co., Ltd.	0.72	0.74	0.75
Shenzhen Yan Tian Port Holdings Co., Ltd.	0.40	0.59	0.53

Source: Wind Financial Terminal, https://www.wind.com.cn/.
a. The exchange rate of the Chinese yuan to the US dollar averaged 0.14493 in 2020.

TABLE 1.5 **World rankings of port operators, 1996–2019**

RANK	1996	2001	2003	2006	2008	2013	2016	2019
1	PSA	HPH[a]	HPH	HPH	HPH	PSA	PSA	PSA
2	HPH	PSA[b]	PSA[c]	PSA	PSA	HPH	HPH	COSCO[d]
3	P&O Ports	APMT[e]	APMT	APMT	APMT	APMT	DPW	APMT
4	Maersk	P&O Ports	P&O Ports	DP World[f]	DP World	DPW	APMT	HPH
5	Sea-Land	Eurogate[g]	Eurogate	COSCO	COSCO	COSCO	COSCO	DP World
6	Eurokai	DPA	COSCO	Eurogate	Eurogate	TIL	China Merchants Ports	China Merchants Ports[h]
7	DPA	Evergreen	Evergreen	SSA Marine	SSA Marine	China Shipping	TIL	TIL
8	ICTSI	COSCO	DPA	APL/NOL	APL/NOL	Hanjin	ICTSI	ICTSI
9	SSA	Hanjin	SSA	HHLA	HHLA	Evergreen	Evergreen	CMA CGM
10	HHLA	APL/NOL	SSA	Hanjin	Hanjin	Eurogate	Eurogate	SSA Marine

Source: Drewry 2021.
Note: Rankings are based on container throughput in twenty-foot equivalent units. Rankings are not adjusted by equity shares in the case of joint ventures.
a. Acquires ECT (Rotterdam); HPH is from Hong Kong SAR, China.
b. Acquires Sinport Sinergie Portuali (Genova).
c. Acquires Hesse Natie and Noordnatie (Antwerp).
d. Acquires Noatum (Spain) and OOCL-operated terminals.
e. Acquires Sea-Land by Maersk, separation of terminal division APMT.
f. DPA becomes DPW and takes over P&O Ports.
g. Acquires Contship Italia and BLG (Bremen).
h. Acquires TCP (Brazil).

TABLE 1.6 **SEZs in China's largest container ports**

RANK	PORT	SEZ INITIATIVE(S)
1	Shanghai	SEZ formed in 1984
2	Ningbo-Zhoushan	Ningbo SEZ formed in 1984; free trade zone established in Zhoushan in 2017
3	Shenzhen	SEZ formed in 1980; China's largest SEZ in foreign trade
4	Guangzhou-Nansha	Guangzhou designated a SEZ in 1984; free trade zone established in Nansha in 2014
5	Qingdao	SEZ formed in 1984
6	Tianjin	SEZ formed in 1984
7	Xiamen	SEZ formed in 1980
8	Dalian	SEZ formed in 1984
9	Yingkou	Free trade zone established in 2017

Source: Drewry 2021.
Note: SEZ = special economic zone.

PORTS AND SPECIAL ECONOMIC ZONES

Chinese ports expanded in tandem with the development of export-oriented special economic zones (SEZs), each located in direct proximity to a port. Four—in Shenzhen, Zhuhai, Shantou, and Xiamen—were established in 1980 and were accompanied by investments in new port facilities. The SEZs had an immediate impact on the national economy. In 1981, the original four zones accounted for 59.8 percent of total foreign direct investment in China, with Shenzhen accounting for 50.6 percent and the other three about 3 percent each. Three years later, the four accounted for 26 percent of China's total foreign direct investment.

In 1984, SEZs were created in 14 coastal port cities, from Dalian to Beihai, triggering development of more port infrastructure, particularly for container ports, which were essential to support the country's export-oriented strategy. Table 1.6 shows the SEZs associated with each of China's 10 largest container ports.

THE EXPANSION OF PORT-HINTERLAND NETWORKS

River ports handle about a third of all Chinese port traffic, with about 3.7 billion tons of cargo transported via inland waterways in 2017. The Yangtze River Basin, the Pearl River Basin, and the Grand Canal are the top three, handling almost all cargo volumes carried on China's inland water transport system (about 60 percent, 17 percent, and 10 percent, respectively) (Aritua et al. 2020). The Yangtze River accounts for more than half of the total river cargo volume. The Suzhou port complex, located in the Yangtze Delta, handled more than 500 million tons of cargo in 2018. The Port of Chongqing, 1,000 nautical miles from the sea, can handle ships of up to 5,000 deadweight tonnage (dwt). Its 2018 throughput was 200 million tons. The Port of Wuhan, 600 nautical miles from the sea, can accommodate oceangoing ships of up to 10,000 dwt. Map 1.2, earlier in this chapter, shows the 10 river ports with the highest cargo throughput in 2018.

TABLE 1.7 **Cargo volumes on China's main waterways, 2017**

WATERWAY	TONS		TON-KILOMETERS	
	MILLIONS	PERCENTAGE OF TOTAL	BILLIONS	PERCENTAGE OF TOTAL
Yangtze River	2,209	59.6	1,091.5	73.3
Pearl River	622	16.8	129.5	8.7
Grand Canal	354	9.6	104.9	7.0
Heilongjiang River Basin	11.9	0.3	0.7	..
Total	3,706	100	1,488.5	100

Source: World Bank.
Note: .. = negligible.

FIGURE 1.11

Length of transport routes of roads, inland waterways, and railways in China, 1978–2018

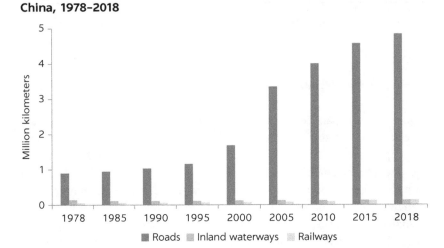

Source: China Waterborne Transport Research Institute (WTI).

As of 2018, the length of the navigable national inland waterway network was 127,126 kilometers. About 52 percent of that is navigable by the smallest commercial vessels. Larger vessels (with more than 1,000-ton loading capacity) can use only 10 percent of the navigable waterways. The Yangtze River system, including its trunk line and tributaries, is the longest of the entire network and the most used for inland water transport (table 1.7). Its inland ports are the largest as measured by throughput. The Huai River and the Pearl River account for more than 25 percent of the navigable waterways. After the Yangtze, the Pearl River is the second most used for cargo transport.

China's government has invested heavily in the country's transport infrastructure. The most significant growth can be seen in highways, with the total length of the highway network growing more than fivefold from 1978 to 2018 (figure 1.11). In contrast, the railway network has grown at only half that rate, and the use of railways to carry freight remains relatively low.

DRY PORTS

One of the major advantages of dry ports is their ability to deliver efficient customs clearance. In 2017, China's national customs administration introduced a new system designed to standardize customs enforcement and improve efficiency nationwide. For dry ports, goods now need to be examined only once before being transferred directly to their destination. Thus, goods being shipped from an inland dry port can clear customs there rather than being reexamined when they reach a coastal port.

Most dry ports also serve as logistics centers, providing customs and inspection services, storage services, issuance and execution of bills of lading, and other services. They also house branches of freight forwarders, shipping agents, and shipping lines that facilitate the receipt of goods, packing of cargo, consolidation of shipments, return of empty containers, and issuance of bills of lading for multimodal shipments having inland dry ports as the origin or destination.

In contrast with Europe and elsewhere, dry ports are a relatively new part of Chinese logistics systems, first appearing in 2002. Their initial development was stimulated by the high costs of inland transport and the desire to extend the benefits of containerization as far inland from ports as possible. Their establishment has made a major contribution to the efficiency of freight transport in China. In addition, they have increased the capacity of coastal ports by providing storage and clearance facilities off-dock, thereby reducing dwell times in seaports. An overview of the location of dry ports is provided in map 1.3 earlier in this chapter.

The example of Yiwu dry port (box 1.3) illustrates the rapid growth of inland ports and their reach into the hinterland.

In recent years, China has focused on expanding the use of railways to move freight into the hinterlands. This expansion is encouraged by the continued construction of inland dry ports, which are often connected to the coastline by rail. Inland river ports drive the use of the inland waterways in transporting freight. The ports that moved the most container volume by rail are listed in table 1.8.

BOX 1.3

Yiwu dry port and the evolution of small-merchandise export inspection

Yiwu is in Zhejiang province in eastern China. An inland city, it has become one of the largest distribution centers in the world for small merchandise and is recognized by the United Nations as the world's largest merchandise transaction market. In 2018, Yiwu achieved a turnover of ¥ 452.3 billion (US$68.2 billion), with a total import and export value of ¥ 256 billion (US$38.6 billion).

To a large extent, Yiwu owes its success to its unique institutional and cultural environment. Nonetheless, the constant improvement of its transport connections within China and globally is an important factor in its success. It was given a boost when China shifted focus from domestic to international trade in 2002. Because the Yiwu market dealt with small merchandise, its shipments had particular "Yiwu characteristics," with one container carrying hundreds of different products. Although this was not a problem for the domestic market, international trade requirements required the filing of hundreds of documents for a single container, with both shippers and freight forwarders needing to repeat the filing of documents at several different customs offices.

To deal with this problem, Yiwu set up a local customs office, which pushed for a specific form of customs inspection for small merchandise exports with Yiwu characteristics. In 2004, the central customs administration approved classifying such exports as "tourism shopping goods." In 2009, Yiwu customs was officially recognized and authorized to carry out inspection of small merchandise on site, the first of its kind in China.

In 2010, the Hangzhou customs office launched the reform of small-merchandise export inspection and testing. In 2011, China customs and Zhejiang province

continued

Box 1.3, *continued*

signed a memorandum of cooperation formally supporting the comprehensive reform of inspections of small-merchandise exports. This was followed by the Three-Year Action Plan formulated by Hangzhou customs, which supported the Yiwu reforms. Finally, in 2013, the customs surveillance area at the inland port of Yiwu was officially approved for operation by Hangzhou customs.

The customs clearance reforms have led to significant improvements in the efficiency of customs inspections at Yiwu. The inspection time for a single container has been shortened from an average of four hours to about five minutes. Vehicle detention time for inspection purposes has been reduced by approximately 30,000 vehicle-hours annually. The reforms permit the maximum value of goods declared in a single shipment to be US$150,000, allowing dozens or even hundreds of commodities in a single container to be declared as a single unit, thus saving significant documentation costs for the enterprises involved.

Covering an area of about 0.7 square kilometer, the dry port consists of customs areas, commodity inspection halls, office buildings, and foreign-trade warehouses. It is connected to several coastal ports, including Shanghai and Ningbo-Zhoushan. It also handles cargo for the China-Europe rail service. The first train from Yiwu to Madrid departed on November 18, 2014. As the origin for China's longest rail route, with a total length of 13,052 kilometers in 2019, it operated an average of two trains per week. Other China-Europe trains currently in operation connect Yiwu to Afghanistan, Belarus, the Czech Republic, the Islamic Republic of Iran, Latvia, the Russian Federation, Spain, and the United Kingdom.

TABLE 1.8 **Top 10 ports in China, by container volume moved by rail-sea transport, 2018**

RANKING (BY VOLUME)	PORT	VOLUME OF CONTAINERS MOVED BY RAIL-SEA TRANSPORT (THOUSAND TEU)	PROPORTION OF TOTAL PORT CONTAINER THROUGHPUT (%)
1	Qingdao	1,153.7	6.0
2	Yingkou	762.7	11.8
3	Ningbo-Zhoushan	601.7	2.3
4	Tianjin	492.4	3.1
5	Dalian	393.4	4.0
6	Lianyungang	302.8	6.4
7	Tangshan	227.0	7.7
8	Shenzhen	110.5	0.4
9	Chongqing	78.4	6.7
10	Guangzhou	64.7	0.3

Source: Shanghai International Shipping Institute.
Note: Shanghai, China's largest port, is missing from this list because of its heavy reliance on inland waterway transport. TEU = twenty-foot equivalent unit.

NOTE

1. At the port level, the LSCI is generated from six components: (1) number of scheduled ship calls per week in the port, (2) total deployed capacity offered at the port, (3) number of regular liner shipping services to and from the port, (4) number of liner shipping companies providing services to and from the port, (5) average size (in TEUs) of the ships deployed by the scheduled service with the largest average vessel size, and (6) number of other ports connected to the port through direct liner shipping services.

REFERENCES

Aritua, Bernard, Lu Cheng, Richard van Liere, and Harrie de Leijer. 2020. *Blue Routes for a New Era*. Washington, DC: World Bank.

China Association of Port-of-Entry. 2020. *China Ports Yearbook 1978–2020*. Beijing: China Customs Press.

Drewry. 2021. *Global Container Terminal Operators Annual Review and Forecast 2021/22*. London: Drewry Research.

IHS Markit. 2019. *Shipping and Shipbuilding Outlook*. https://ihsmarkit.com/info /0219/2019-shipping-shipbuilding-outlook.html.

Ministry of Transport. 2018. "Statistical Bulletin on Development of China's Transportation Industry." 交通运输行业发展统计公报 (in Chinese). Beijing. https://xxgk.mot.gov.cn/2020 /jigou/zhghs/202006/t20200630_3321179.html.

Ministry of Transport. 2019. *40 years of China's Opening-Up and Reform*. Beijing: Ministry of Transport.

National Bureau of Statistics of China. 2020. *China Port Yearbook*. China Statistics Press. http://www.stats.gov.cn/tjsj/ndsj/2020/indexeh.htm.

UNCTAD (United Nations Conference on Trade and Development). 2020. *Review of Maritime Transport 2019*. New York: United Nations Publications. https://unctad.org/system/files /official-document/rmt2019_en.pdf.

World Bank. 2021. "The Container Port Performance Index 2020: A Comparable Assessment of Container Port Performance." World Bank, Washington, DC.

Ye, Shilin, Xinhua Qi, and Yecheng Xu. 2020. "Analyzing the Relative Efficiency of China's Yangtze River Port System." *Maritime Economics & Logistics* 22 (4): 640–60.

2 Reforming and Developing China's Port Sector

INTRODUCTION

The previous chapter demonstrates that China has managed to develop its ports successfully over the past 40 years. This chapter describes the policy decisions and reforms that enabled this development.

The policy and reform context for China's port sector can be framed in several ways (Cullinane and Wang 2006; Notteboom and Yang 2017; Xu and Chin 2012). Table 2.1 distinguishes four periods, each approximately a decade long and commencing with an important economic event that affected port policy.

Port development is affected by a variety of public sector activities, such as trade facilitation, spatial planning, and investments in infrastructure. It is impossible to describe all relevant policies in detail. Thus, this chapter presents only the major policy initiatives in the four periods and for the following eight policy dimensions:

- China's integrated macroeconomic development approach
- Regional economic development policies
- Port governance and reform
- Financing investments in port infrastructure
- Planning and development of ports and port cities
- Hinterland transport policies
- Environmental policies
- Policies for upgrading skills and technological capabilities.

The major policy initiatives, by time period and policy dimension, are summarized in table 2.2 and described in greater detail in the sections that follow.

CHINA'S APPROACH TO MACROECONOMIC DEVELOPMENT

China, now the world's largest manufacturer and exporter, was not integrated within the world economy before 1978. Internally, individual regions did not have efficient exchanges, competition, or connections with markets at home or abroad. The five-year economic and social development plans of the 1980s

TABLE 2.1 **Phases in China's port development and key reforms during those phases, 1978–present**

PHASE	KEY EVENT	PORT SECTOR FOCUS
1978–91	Official reform and opening of China's planned economy system	• Increasing port capacity • Increasing sources of financing for port construction projects
1992–2001	Formal establishment of China's socialist market economic system	• Increasing port capacity • Motivating local government participation
2002–11	China joins the World Trade Organization	• Complete decentralization of the port industry
2012–present	Structural shift of China's economy from export-led to domestic demand	• Port resource integration • High quality vs. focus on high capacity

Source: World Bank.

TABLE 2.2 **Major policy initiatives, 1978–present**

POLICY AREA	1978–91	1992–2001	2002–11	2012–PRESENT
Macroeconomic development approach	Reform and opening of China's planned economy, enabling private and corporate wealth creation; open-door policy aimed at trade growth.	Export-led economic development of China's socialist market economic system.	Expansion of international trade following accession to the World Trade Organization; reduced regional economic disparities; economic stimulus program (World Bank 2020).	Focus on sustainable development and growth, in large part based on growing domestic demand. Goal of innovation-driven economic growth.
Regional economic development	Development of the first four SEZs along the coast. Special status for 14 port cities as "coastal open cities."	Investments in infrastructure and special zones as engines for growth (with a focus on Shenzhen SEZ). Development of additional SEZs in inland provinces.	Implementation of Go West policy[a] to develop China's interior provinces, among others, through large-scale investments in infrastructure and inland logistics hubs.	Development of the Belt and Road Initiative, with additional focus on rail routes across Asia to Europe.
Port governance and reform	Steps toward decentralization and commercialization of port development, previously under sole control of central government. Freedom for cargo owners to build port facilities. Policy to allow foreign entry in terminal operations under strict conditions.	Continuation of decentralization and commercialization. Separation of administrative functions in public agencies and commercial port enterprises. Tests of public-private initiatives via joint ventures.	Complete transfer of port development to local governments (in 2004 Port Law). Relaxation of conditions for foreign entry, mainly by allowing operators to independently set prices.	Formation of provincial port groups (with encouragement of central government) to prevent excessive competition among local port enterprises, with associated risks of overcapacity. Investments by port companies in inland port networks encouraged by central government.
Investments in and financing of port infrastructure	Focus on creating additional capacity. Huge public investments in port infrastructure. Gradual growth of additional financing mechanisms, including bank loans. User charges (dubbed "port construction fees") levied on importers and exporters.	Ongoing focus on expanding port capacity. More responsibility of port enterprises for financing port development. First listings of port enterprises on stock markets.	Expectation that port enterprises generate vast majority of finance required for port development through operating income, equity financing, and bond financing. Foreign investments take shape.	Policies promoting mergers of port enterprises to form regional port groups and policies encouraging investments in hinterland networks by port groups.

continued

TABLE 2.2, *continued*

POLICY AREA	1978–91	1992–2001	2002–11	2012–PRESENT
Planning and development of ports and port cities	Regional and city governments promote port development by designating land for port activities and providing tax advantages for port activities.	Continued support for port development, for example, by granting land for port development to municipal port companies.	Cities enable port relocation through land exchanges to enable growth, reduce negative environmental and transportation impacts, and free up space for urban waterfront development.	Policies to reduce negative impacts of port activities on port cities, notably to improve sustainability of port-related transport flows (freight and passengers).
Hinterland transport	Development and execution of transportation plans for individual transport modes. Construction of hinterland infrastructure. Develop key rail connections for major northern ports for coal transportation.	Policies to encourage development of inland ports and create partnerships to invest in construction of high-capacity, high-speed, multilane highways, and inland ports using commercial principles.	Roll-out of National Trunk Highway System, connecting all provincial capitals and cities with at least 200,000 residents. Liberalization of road haulage. Ambitious national plans for expanding rail freight capacity. Rapid development of dry ports.	Integrated development of freight corridors and regional multimodal transport hubs. Policy goal to shift freight away from roads, mainly by improving rail access to ports. Promotion of China-Europe cargo trains, especially from inland industrial centers in China.
Environment	No environmental policies specifically aimed at ports.	No environmental policies specifically aimed at ports.	Goal of 10 percent reduction in emissions of major pollutants under 11th Five-Year Plan (2006–10).	High priority for green transportation under 12th and 13th Five-Year Plans. Ambitious Green Port program launched by Ministry of Transportation.
Upgrading skills and technological capabilities	Skill development by maritime universities. New employee contracts with performance-based wage levels in port enterprises. Initial efforts for a shared approach to transport-related ICT systems, including those for ports.	Launch of electronic data interchange projects to automate, digitize, process, and transmit documents related to all aspects of container transport.	Policies to develop comprehensive information sharing by ports, customs, hinterland transport modes, government, logistics service providers, and cargo owners.	Large-scale funding of scientific research, focus on promoting innovation. Focus on use of ICT to enhance productivity and sustainability. Development of fully automated container terminals and transport chains.

Source: World Bank.

Note: ICT = information and communication technology; SEZ = special economic zone.

a. The 12 priority provinces of the Go West program were Chongqing, Sichuan, Guizhou, Yunnan, Tibet, Shaanxi, Gansu, Ningxia, Xinjiang, Inner Mongolia, Guangxi, and Qinghai.

prioritized the coastal provinces for industrialization, and the central government devised special policy measures to help export-oriented sectors leverage cheap labor, finance, and proximity to markets for the purpose of integrating coastal industries into global value chains.

These macroeconomic trends were accelerated by China's accession to the World Trade Organization in 2001. A surge in consumer demand in the United States, Europe, and the emerging economies created an opportunity for China's exporting industries, which in turn catalyzed domestic reforms. These reforms brought greater competitiveness in the global market and closer integration with the world economy (Hofman 2018). Export-led growth also accentuated regional disparities, given that foreign trade and related productivity gains were heavily concentrated on China's east coast.

In the late 1990s, the 10 coastal provinces and municipalities were home to 10 percent of the Chinese population but generated about half of China's gross domestic product (GDP). The ensuing Go West program of geographic rebalancing, adopted in 2000, aimed to fuel the economic growth of the 12 central and western provinces through direct fiscal transfers, tax preferences, and expanded development finance. When China's labor surplus began to shrink in 2010, soaring wage rates on the coast pushed industries to relocate to less-urbanized central regions, where the costs of labor and land were lower (Lemoine et al. 2014). This trend was compounded by the contraction of international trade in the aftermath of the 2008 global financial crisis. In response, the central government launched an economic stimulus plan, with most expenditures being directed inland. These internal and external factors led to the center of gravity of China's growth shifting inward at an accelerated pace, causing productivity to converge across regions and regional disparities to narrow.

Since 2006, the foreign trade of the central region has grown at an average rate of 17.2 percent annually, 8.2 percentage points higher than the national average. At the end of 2017, the region's foreign trade was valued at US$236.77 billion (6 percent of China's total foreign trade value).

China's rapid economic growth has also been fueled by steady urbanization over the past three decades. By 2020, the country's urban population had quintupled, reaching 60 percent of the total population (from 19 percent in 1980). The spatial transformation of the country occurred together with sectoral transformation of the economy—about half a billion rural residents moved to urban areas to seek jobs in manufacturing and services in special economic zones (SEZs) and export-oriented industries (World Bank 2020). Consequently, the first cities to capture economies of scale and specialization during China's export-led growth were on the coast or close to waterways leading to international waters. Growing cities became increasingly connected with each other and with the rest of the world, further increasing productivity through agglomeration effects.

From 2010 on, China started to rebalance its economy toward services and innovation, shifting from a resource- and energy-intensive growth pattern to more efficient use of resources (World Bank and Development Research Center of the State Council of the People's Republic of China 2014). The concept of ecological civilization endorsed by the central government in 2015 provided a framework for adjustments to China's development pattern in the medium to longer term, including low-carbon growth, green development, pollution reduction, and development of a circular economy[1] (Hanson 2019). China's most recent five-year plans give due consideration to key areas of policy and regulation, finance, and institutional and technological innovation (box 2.1).

REGIONAL ECONOMIC DEVELOPMENT POLICIES AND THEIR IMPACT ON THE PORT SECTOR

China's regional economic development policies have deeply affected port development. The main policy instrument in the early stages of China's development was the establishment of SEZs to attract foreign direct investment, expand China's exports, and accelerate the infusion of new technology.

SEZs are typically served by specific infrastructure such as roads, power, and water. The basic concept includes the following characteristics: (1) a

BOX 2.1

Port development under China's 11th, 12th, 13th, and 14th Five-Year Plans

11th Five-Year Plan (2006–10)

- Build equipment to handle large ships, including container ships carrying more than 10,000 standard containers.
- Optimize the layout of coastal and river ports.
- Increase ports' throughput capacity.
- Construct bulk goods and container transport systems at major coastal ports.

12th Five-Year Plan (2011–15)

- Modernize coastal port groups.
- Construct more coal, crude oil, iron ore, and container terminals at coastal ports.
- Construct about 440 berths for ships weighing 10,000 tons or more.
- Deepen the integration of port and coast resources and optimize port layouts.

13th Five-Year Plan (2016–20)

- Improve and upgrade clusters of ports in the Bohai Sea Rim, Yangtze River Delta, and Pearl River Delta based on coordination and division of work.
- Construct international shipping centers at major harbor cities.
- Construct specialized berths for containers, crude oil, and liquefied natural gas at coastal harbors.
- Increase the level of intelligent systems used in harbors.
- Improve port transport and distribution systems.
- Establish a new model of coordinated oversight of maritime affairs.

14th Five-Year Plan (2021–25)

- Standardize and reduce port and shipping charges.
- Increase synergies between port clusters.
- Promote integrated governance of the Yangtze River Delta port cluster.
- Coordinate the functional layout of ports and airports in the Guangdong–Hong Kong SAR, China–Macao SAR, China greater bay area.
- Promote connectivity to create a new international land and sea trade corridor.

Sources: Ministry of Transport 2007a, 2011, 2017, 2022.

geographically delimited area, (2) a single management or administration, (3) benefits based on physical location within the zone, and (4) a separate customs area (duty-free benefits) and streamlined procedures (World Bank 2009).

Of the several types of SEZs in China, the following are particularly relevant to port sector development.

- *National economic and technological development zones.* By 1984, after the early success of the first four SEZs (Shantou, Shenzhen, Xiamen, and Zhuhai) had been confirmed, China resolved to open its economy further by extending similar favorable policies to 14 "coastal open cities." Legally, these zones are now officially known as economic and technological development zones (ETDZs) (China Internet Information Center, n.d.). Within ETDZs, national export-processing zones can be developed.
- *Bonded zones.* Bonded zones run by the customs authorities were introduced in 1990. Bonded port areas date from 2005; bonded logistics zones from 2013. Their areas are quite small and they are nearly always located within an SEZ (Herlevi 2016).
- *Free trade zones.* Free trade zones were established in areas with geographical advantages for trade, such as major seaports and international airports.

The first was approved in Shanghai in 2013. Three more free trade zones were approved in 2015 and another seven in 2017, followed by one in 2018, six in 2019, and three in 2020. Each of the twenty-one zones is named for the province or municipality where it is located.

In addition to the SEZs created by the central government, many prefecture-level and county-level development zones have been established since the 1990s. In 2019, China had 219 national ETDZs, 169 national high-technology industrial development zones, 17 national border economic cooperation zones, 63 national export-processing zones, 66 bonded zones, 21 national free trade zones (as of 2020), and more than 1,000 provincial SEZs. The numbers continue to grow.

There have been three generations of SEZs since 1980. As noted, the first generation consisted of the four formed in 1980 in Shantou, Shenzhen, Xiamen, and Zhuhai. These zones encompassed large areas within which the objective was to pursue pragmatic and open economic policies, serving as a testing ground for innovative policies that, if proven effective, would be implemented more widely across the country. The emphasis on forward links with the world, especially through liberalization of foreign investment and trade with capitalist countries, and backward links with other parts of China was part of the rationale for their establishment.

The four SEZs created in 1980 are similar in legal structure to ETDZs, the difference being one of scale (Zeng 2012). The comprehensive SEZs span an entire city or province. From 1984 to 1988, 14 ETDZs were established in coastal cities, and later in cities in the Pearl River Delta, the Yangtze River Delta, and the Min Delta in Fujian. In 1988, the entire province of Hainan was designated as the fifth comprehensive SEZ. In 1992, the government opened 11 border cities and 6 ports along the Yangtze River. Map 2.1 shows the development of the first generation of SEZs.

MAP 2.1

The first generation of special economic zones in China, 1980–92

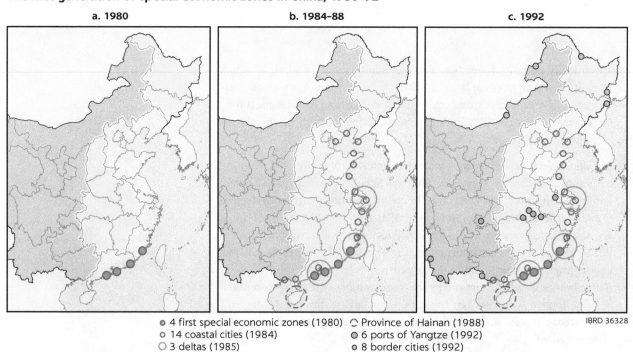

| a. 1980 | b. 1984–88 | c. 1992 |

- ⊙ 4 first special economic zones (1980) ◌ Province of Hainan (1988)
- ○ 14 coastal cities (1984) ◉ 6 ports of Yangtze (1992)
- ○ 3 deltas (1985) ◉ 8 border cities (1992)

IBRD 36328

Source: World Bank 2009, 254.

The second generation of SEZs, such as the Shanghai Pudong New Area and Tianjin Binhai New Area, were developed in a different context, though based on the experience of the first generation. From 1992 to 1994, the State Council launched a second round of national ETDZ establishment, during which 18 new development zones were approved. Regional development became a central goal of this generation of ETDZs, which were designed to develop new strategic growth poles and thereby to trigger a diffusion effect. An additional objective was to stimulate knowledge-intensive and technology-intensive industries. The third generation of SEZs, those established after 2000, were issue oriented. For example, the Chengdu-Chongqing pilot zone focuses on coordinated urban-rural development.

Overall, SEZs have had a positive effect on China's economic development, trade, and technological development (see Wang 2013; Wei 2000; Wu, Jiuli, and Chong 2021; Yeung, Lee, and Kee 2013; Zeng 2011, 2015). The first four had an almost immediate impact. In 1981, they accounted for 59.8 percent of total foreign direct investment in China, with Shenzhen accounting for the lion's share (50.6 percent) and the other three about 3 percent each. Three years later, the four SEZs still accounted for 26 percent of China's total foreign direct investment (Yeung, Lee, and Kee 2013). Shenzhen developed from a small town with 30,000 inhabitants in 1980 to 800,000 inhabitants in 1988 and 7 million in 2000. The new residents include the best-trained professionals in the country, attracted by high salaries, better housing, and educational opportunities for their children. During this period, GDP per capita grew more than 60-fold (World Bank 2009). Regions within China with multiple SEZs have enjoyed greater economic growth than those having only one. Furthermore, the regions where SEZs were established early on have experienced greater economic benefits than regions where they were created later (Crane et al. 2018).

The huge impact of the SEZs and the resultant widening of regional disparities—with much greater development in coastal regions—prompted the designation of SEZs in the capital cities of all interior provinces and autonomous regions. Yet poor accessibility of these SEZs to foreign markets limited development of the interior provinces until the 2000s, when the Chinese government introduced its Go West policies. Those policies included huge infrastructure investments and the Belt and Road Initiative, which aims, among other things, to improve the international connectivity of China's interior regions through better rail connections between China, the Central Asian countries, and Europe.

China's more recent regional development policies have focused on forming urban agglomerations. The designation of an area as an urban agglomeration affects its ability to attract economic activities. To obtain urban agglomeration status, city clusters are evaluated on the basis of seven quantitative criteria and nine specific indicators (including number of cities, number of cities with a population of more than a million, overall population size, urbanization level, GDP per capita, economic density, and the ratio of agricultural to nonagricultural output). The twenty urban agglomerations identified to date fall into three categories: five of national-level importance, which receive top construction priority; nine of regional-level importance that require stable investment and support; and six local urban agglomerations, mostly in the interior provinces, that require significant support because they have not fully developed into urban agglomerations yet. Most of China's urban agglomerations lie within well-established transport corridors providing port access (map 2.2).

MAP 2.2
Spatial pattern of China's urbanization based on "clusters along the axes"

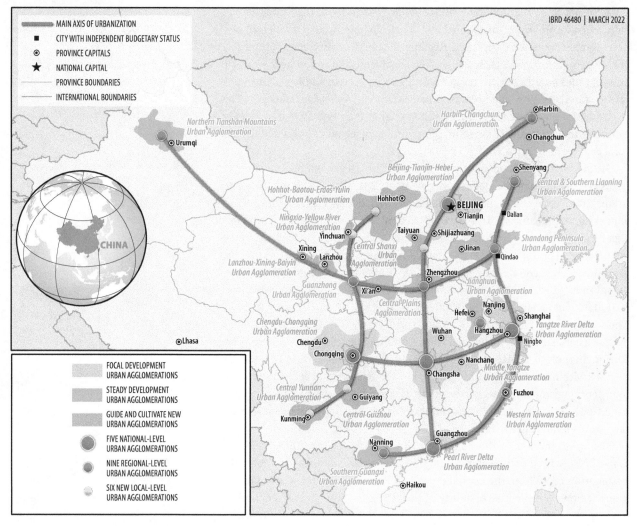

Source: Fang 2015. © Fang Chuanglin. Used with the permission of Fang Chuanglin. Further permission required for reuse.

PORT GOVERNANCE AND REFORM

China's port governance has evolved very differently from that of most other countries. The current governance model reflects the continued central government perception of ports as an instrument of macroeconomic strategy, combined with a realization of the importance of decentralized day-to-day management of port operations and private operators' need to make a sustainable return on their investment. The initial governance model prioritized economic development and internationalization; these priorities were later modified to give greater consideration to the financial, operational, and environmental sustainability of the ports themselves, and to reduce socioeconomic disparities between coastal and inland regions. China's model contrasts with the landlord port model adopted elsewhere, which places less emphasis on macroeconomic and socioeconomic strategies and relies more on a balance between interport competition and regulation to ensure that national objectives are achieved.

The Chinese model gives the central government ultimate control over port development. Private companies act as service providers (as in the landlord port model), but port enterprises are state-owned enterprises (SOEs) that follow the broad direction set out in the five-year plans. For instance, the SOEs increasingly invest in innovation and technology and have developed ambitious environmental initiatives, in line with the current five-year plan. Some countries may find China's governance context inapplicable but may still learn useful lessons despite the differences.

State ownership of port enterprises has ensured that their actions and investments supported development strategies, both within and beyond the port gate, in a manner consistent with broad macroeconomic and social policies. It is not self-evident that such coordination is dependent on who owns and operates port assets, but in a relatively weak legal and contractual environment, coordination within the state sector was arguably easier than it would have been under a public-private partnership model. Port SOEs have also benefited from implicit government guarantees when raising funding, enabling them to finance their rapid expansion at relatively low cost. Strong human resource and management practices have ensured that port SOEs remain performance oriented and have incentives to adopt new technologies and business practices.

Before 1978, China's port sector was heavily centralized. Port ownership and governance were under the control of the Ministry of Transport (MoT), which combined regulatory, administrative, and operational functions within a single entity. Local government had no control over ports, and all revenues accrued to the central government (Cullinane and Wang 2006). The MoT oversaw all ships entering and leaving, and directly managed each port. Although other government agencies were involved (for example, customs and police), they had no say in port operations or development.

After 1971, China's foreign trade began to grow. However, capacity at the ports was insufficient to deal with the growth. Though port capacity increased, it was not able to keep up with demand, partly because of ineffective port governance. Centrally funded local port bureaus exercised both administrative and enterprise functions,[2] but their funding was not linked to port performance (Qiu 2008). As a result, ports had little incentive to improve their efficiency or the quality of the services offered, resulting in severe capacity problems even though the total volume handled was relatively small (for example, 280 million tons in 1978) (Notteboom and Yang 2017). Figure 2.1 offers a schematic view of port governance between 1978 and 1983.

A reform process began in 1984: 14 coastal cities were opened for international trade and foreign direct investment. A pilot project was set up in Tianjin to test a devolved structure in which the MoT controlled strategic planning, port development, financing, and high-level regulation, while the local government became responsible for day-to-day management.

The pilot was expanded and led to the decentralization of other ports, placing them (except for Qinhuangdao) under joint management. Ports became autonomously operated enterprises owned by the state (either central or local) and based on profit-sharing principles. Central financing was linked to port performance.

As part of the reform, the MoT implemented a policy whereby "whoever builds will own and benefit," encouraging corporate, municipal, and provincial initiatives to build and manage port facilities. This era marked the first time

FIGURE 2.1
China's port governance model, 1978–83

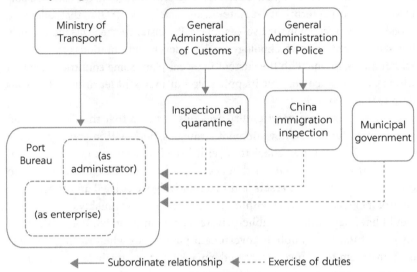

Source: World Bank.

since 1949 that nonministerial entities could invest in berths and terminals within ports under the control of the MoT. The reform was a major step. Under the new system (figure 2.2), municipal governments oversaw human resources, while the MoT retained control of port infrastructure, development, and procurement (Guan and Yahalom 2011). The central government also retained national-level regulatory, policy-making, and planning powers. Port authorities were granted local regulatory powers and SOE status, which pushed them to become more market oriented. Moreover, a new financing structure was developed in which individual ports could keep a certain percentage of their profits for reinvestment, as long as they covered their costs under a nationwide price-setting scheme and reached throughput targets set by the MoT (Qiu 2008). The agreement linked the availability of investment funds to port performance, providing incentives for the improvement of operational efficiency.[3]

However, even though the Chinese seaport system was moving toward a decentralized governance model, the joint management system remained dominated by the central government. The MoT was still in charge of procurement and financing; port development and innovation projects required MoT approval; and the ministry received the lion's share of revenues from port operations. Local governments could participate only in the planning and construction of new terminals and provide assistance through the supply of materials and logistics.

But ports were not expanding at the pace expected by the central government. As a result, port development was pushed to the top of the government's agenda in subsequent five-year plans. Further efforts were made to decentralize. In 1992, the central government issued several circulars calling for reform, and attempts were made to strip port authorities of many of their administrative functions so that the ports could become full-fledged business entities (State Council 1992). However, the success of these efforts was limited because

FIGURE 2.2

China's port governance model, 1984–91

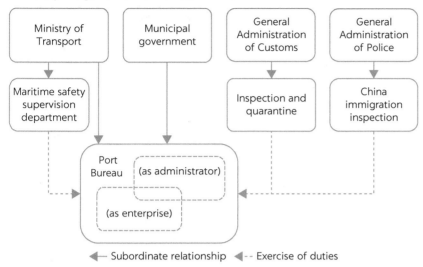

Source: World Bank.

of their complexity (Cullinane and Wang 2006). In November 1992, the Maritime Code laid down a legal structure for the sector. Among other points, it stated that all maritime spaces and surface transport modes (except rail) would fall under the remit of the MoT, which would be responsible for formulating maritime and national port planning policies. The MoT also issued several opinions on deepening reforms, accelerating traffic growth, and making faster progress in the construction and operation of public berths and cargo owners' private wharves. The reforms included the introduction of commercial management at the terminal level. New corporations and private entities were invited to build and operate public terminals and special wharves. Through joint ventures, international groups such as Hutchison Whampoa (Hong Kong SAR, China), PSA (Singapore), and AP Møller (Denmark) started operating new container terminals in several Chinese seaports. As these groups brought in advanced equipment, modern management skills, adherence to international standards, financing, and—in some cases—clients, their entrance put pressure on the Chinese authorities to undertake further market-oriented reforms.

To clear these bottlenecks, further efforts were made to reform port governance in China, through the release in 2001 of a policy entitled Opinions on Deepening the Reform of the Port Management System under the Direct and Dual Leadership of the Central Government (State Council 2001). This policy set out two principles (Wang 2018). First, part of the administrative function would be transferred from each local port enterprise to a relevant government department. Second, municipal government units in host cities were given a stronger say in determining port strategies. Then, in 2001, the MoT issued a notice to "improve the separation of public and private sectors and promote administrative efficiency" (Ministry of Transport 2001). This notice pushed for further decentralization and the separation of the public and private sectors, requiring port enterprises to become economic entities with an independent legal existence. By early 2003, only 11 of 38 ports had completely separated their administrative functions from their port enterprises. So, in March 2003, the

MoT issued a mandate to accelerate the separation of government and port enterprises and strengthen port administration (Ministry of Transport 2003).

Port assets were transferred to municipal governments, and the port bureaus, formerly unitary and funded by the central government, were split into two separate bodies responsible for the administrative and commercial aspects of each port. Local governments set up new units to oversee port administration, while operational functions and assets were assumed by new business enterprises created by the local government. Together, these policies changed the structure of port governance, as shown in figure 2.3.

The central government's full endorsement of these reforms was highlighted by the passing of the Port Law of 2004 and the related Rules on Port Operation and Management (State Council 2004b). These pivotal steps further limited government intervention in port operations and management. They also opened the way to corporatization.

As commercial business entities, port enterprises competed with each other. Although the MoT still managed port planning and regulation at the national and regional levels, the individual port enterprises had assumed control over local port planning (Bury and Leung 2020). The transportation departments of the provincial governments were responsible for strategic planning and policy development at the provincial level, although these efforts had to be consistent with national guidelines developed by the MoT and required approval from the central government. Within this policy framework, local port enterprises were in control of port development and daily port operations.

By 2012, the decentralization of port governance had been largely achieved. However, intense competition between port cities, combining low costs and low tariffs, had resulted in an excess of port capacity (Wang et al. 2020; Xing, Liu, and Chen 2018). The overcapacity coincided with the trend away from international exports, with the economy becoming more domestically driven. Thus, starting

FIGURE 2.3

China's port governance model, 2001–11

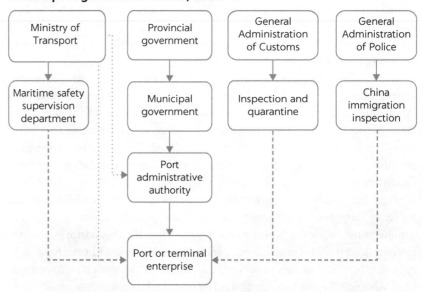

Source: World Bank.

MAP 2.3
Integration of port groups

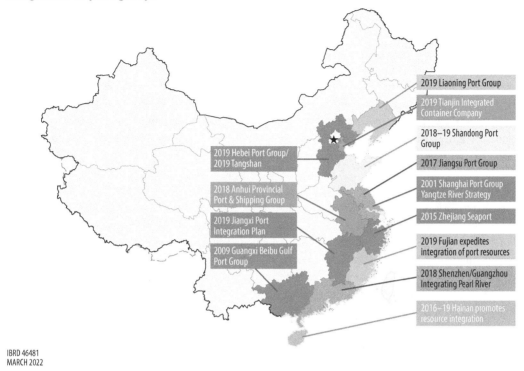

2019 Liaoning Port Group

2019 Tianjin Integrated
Container Company

2018–19 Shandong Port
Group

2017 Jiangsu Port Group

2001 Shanghai Port Group
Yangtze River Strategy

2015 Zhejiang Seaport

2019 Fujian expedites
integration of port resources

2018 Shenzhen/Guangzhou
Integrating Pearl River

2016–19 Hainan promotes
resource integration

2019 Hebei Port Group/
2019 Tangshan

2018 Anhui Provincial
Port & Shipping Group

2019 Jiangxi Port
Integration Plan

2009 Guangxi Beibu Gulf
Port Group

IBRD 46481
MARCH 2022

Source: World Bank, based on data from the China Waterborne Transport Research Institute (WTI).

about 2012, the central government encouraged the formation of provincial port groups to strengthen cooperation and the sharing of resources.

Government efforts to increase coordination and cooperation among ports were articulated in 2014 with the National Development No. 32 plan (State Council 2014). This document called for the integration of port-related transport systems into overall urban planning, encouraged enterprises to develop inland ports, and warned against the unnecessary duplication of port facilities. Also in 2014, the MoT encouraged regional integration by urging ports within the same province to merge. The principle of "one port, one administration," set forth in the 2004 Port Law, would now be realized at the provincial level rather than the city level. By the end of 2019, 10 port groups operated across China—those of Liaoning, Hebei, Shandong, Jiangsu, Zhejiang, Fujian, Guangxi Beibu Gulf, Hainan, Jiangxi, and Anhui (map 2.3 and box 2.2). These groups cover approximately 85 percent of coastal port throughput.

DIVERSIFYING THE FINANCING OF PORT INFRASTRUCTURE

In parallel with the reform of port governance, mechanisms for port financing have undergone a series of changes to diversify the financing channels available to ports. Before the 1980s, the MoT was responsible for financing most port construction and development. Investments by the central government accounted for 80 percent of the capital spent on coastal port construction. This single

BOX 2.2

Port consolidation: The Shanghai International Port Group and its "Yangtze Strategy"

The Shanghai International Port Group (SIPG) is worth highlighting. The "Yangtze Strategy" undertaken by SIPG preceded any state-led initiative toward port consolidation. SIPG's strategy led to investment in several ports along the Yangtze River: the Port of Chongqing, the Port of Wuhan, and the Port of Nanjing.

The purpose of the investment was to create a Yangtze River shipping network. By using the Port of Shanghai as a hub and connecting to feeder ports via a network of inland waterways, SIPG was able to extend market coverage inland. As of 2020, SIPG had invested in 12 port and terminal companies along the river (table B2.2.1). Through these long-term equity investments, SIPG built a logistics system that serves the economic development of the Yangtze River Basin.

In a similar way, though on a much smaller scale, the Port of Ningbo-Zhoushan invested in a container terminal in the Port of Taicang and acquired a 40 percent stake in the Jiangyin Sunan container terminal. The ports of Shanghai and Ningbo-Zhoushan are jointly developing the north side of Xiaoyangshan port; smaller container berths for feeder services from ports along the Yangtze River and some smaller coastal ports will be built to improve the connectivity of Yangshan terminal and strengthen its trans-shipping function.

TABLE B2.2.1 Investments by SIPG in port and terminal companies

RIVER SEGMENT	PORT	COMPANY	SIPG'S SHAREHOLDING POSITION (%)
Downstream	Suzhou	SIPG Zhenghe Container Terminal Co. Ltd., Taicang Port	45.00
	Ningbo-Zhoushan	Ningbo Zhoushan Port Co. Ltd.	5.10
	Wuhu	Wuhu Port Co. Ltd.	35.00
	Jiangyin	Jiangyin Sunan International Container Terminal Co. Ltd.	12.20
	Nanjing	Nanjing Port Co. Ltd.	10.28
	Yancheng	Yancheng SIPG International Port Co. Ltd.	10.00
Midstream	Wuhan	Midstream Wuhan Port Container Co. Ltd.	5.10
	Wuhan	Wuhan Port Group Co. Ltd.	30.00
	Chenglingji	Hunan Chenglingji International Port Group Co. Ltd.	25.00
Upstream	Chongqing	Chongqing International Container Terminal Co. Ltd.	35.00
	Chongqing	Chongqing Orchard Container Terminal Co. Ltd.	35.00
	Yibin	Yibin Port International Container Terminal Co. Ltd.	30.00

Source: China Waterborne Transport Research Institute (WTI).
Note: SIPG = Shanghai International Port Group.

funding mechanism impeded port expansion, which could not keep pace with the growing volume of trade.

To overcome the funding constraints, a number of policies were enacted with the objectives of relieving the central government's budget constraints, giving SOEs more autonomy and financial independence, and attracting foreign capital (Guan and Yahalom 2011). With the implementation of the dual-management system in 1984, funding from the MoT was no longer designated as a grant, but instead became a "government loan" that ports were expected to repay from their revenues.[4] While the MoT remained responsible for procurement and financing,

BOX 2.3

The World Bank's first loans to Guangzhou, Shanghai, and Tianjin

On November 2, 1982, the World Bank approved its first loan of US$124 million to China's port sector. In line with the country's five-year plan, the project targeted the ports of Shanghai, Tianjin, and Huangpu (in the city of Guangzhou). The objectives included the following:

• Creation of additional port capacity to avoid congestion
• Development by the government of a long-term national port strategy
• Initiation of a strategic dialogue based on three studies included in the project.

The main objective of the five-year national economic development plan for the period 1982–86 was to promote investments in the transport sector that would prevent the sector from becoming a serious bottleneck to the country's economic development,

with the understanding that ports had a special position not only in the transfer of resources between northern and southern China, but also as gateways to foreign markets and to foreign sources of plant, equipment, and technology. The government had indicated that coal-handling facilities in Huangpu and container handling facilities in Huangpu, Shanghai, and Tianjin would be accorded high priority for the period (World Bank 1982).

Following this initial project, the World Bank continued to invest in these three ports until 2000: Tianjin Port Project (fiscal 1986, US$130 million); Huangpu Port Project (fiscal 1988, US$88 million); Ningbo and Shanghai Ports Project (fiscal 1989, US$46.4 million for Shanghai Port); Shanghai Port Restructuring and Development Project (fiscal 1993, US$150 million); and China Container Transport Project (fiscal 1999, US$71 million).

Source: World Bank.

---

ports were given increased autonomy in managing their business affairs. Tax incentives were developed to attract both domestic and foreign investment in port construction. Foreign aid (for example, World Bank loans; box 2.3) was also pursued by the central government. Changes in port financing followed a trial-and-error approach, with several revisions made over the years—related, for example, to dealing with foreign investment and construction fees.

By 2003, central government investment had decreased to about 11 percent of the amount that ports required. Needing other sources of financing, port enterprises (including state-owned, foreign-funded, and private enterprises) pursued equity financing, bond financing, and bank loans. By 2013, the proportion of self-raised funds stood at 70 percent of total port construction investment. In 2016, the proportion of bank loans stood at 25 percent, compensating for the continuous decline of central government investment to about 5 percent in 2016.

As can be seen in figure 2.4, the rapid increase in investments went hand in hand with an equally rapid increase in cargo volumes, indicating that the newly developed capacity was soon utilized. Figure 2.5 shows the introduction of new financing sources over time.

In the 1990s, with the transformation of port enterprises into commercial operations, some of the most profitable entities, ranging from shipping companies to port operators, began to list on the capital markets to increase access to funding. The China Merchants Group (CMG), China Ocean Shipping Co. (COSCO), Tianjin Port Development, and the Port of Dalian were all listed on the Hong Kong SAR, China, stock market by 1992. Port enterprises also were listed on the stock exchanges of Shanghai and Shenzhen. The joint-stock system

FIGURE 2.4
Investment levels in China's port sector, 1978–2020

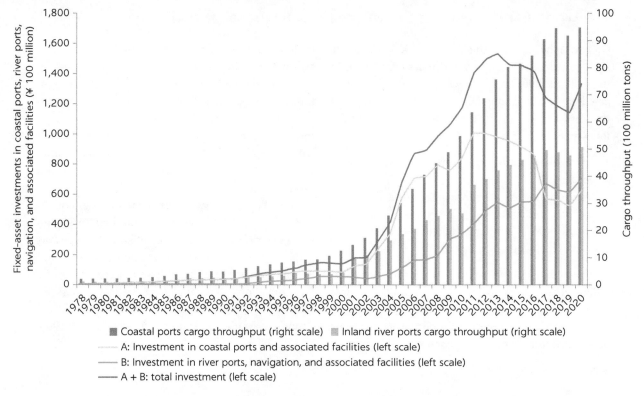

Sources: China Transport Statistical Bulletin (2000–20), https://www.mot.gov.cn/shuju/; Ministry of Transport 2018; China Waterborne Transport Research Institute (WTI).

FIGURE 2.5
Evolution of financing sources for China's port sector, 1978–2020

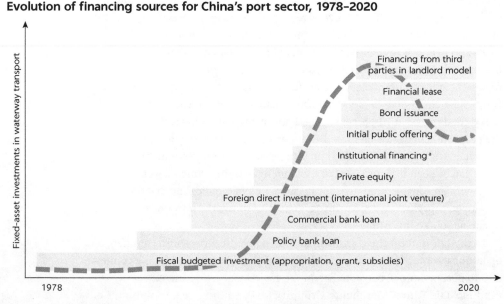

Source: Original analysis conducted for this report by PricewaterhouseCoopers (PwC).
a. Institutional financing refers to financing from institutional investors such as pension fund managers, insurance companies, and so on, rather than from international financial institutions.

FIGURE 2.6

Funding sources for investments in port infrastructure and facilities

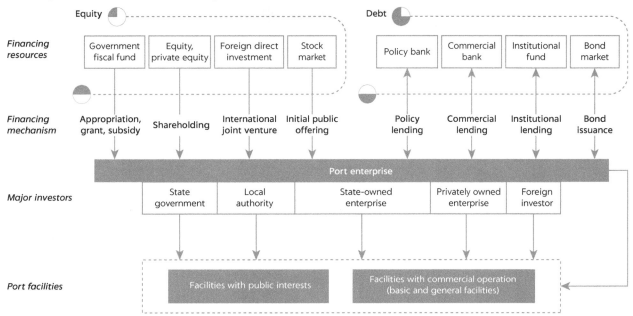

Source: Original analysis conducted for this report by PricewaterhouseCoopers (PwC).

and listings made it possible for companies such as CMG and COSCO to set up their subsidiaries as container terminal operators, CM Ports and COSCO-Pacific, respectively. By 2000, nine port enterprises were listed on the Shanghai and Shenzhen stock exchanges, including Chiwan (a port area in western Shenzhen), Shekou (also in western Shenzhen), Yantian (eastern Shenzhen), Yuefuhua (in the Port of Zhuhai, Guangdong), Beihai Xinli (Northern Bay Port), Shanggang container terminal (Port of Shanghai), the Port of Jinzhou (in Liaoning province), the Port of Tianjin, and the Port of Xiamen.

Figure 2.6 illustrates the financing resources available for port enterprises. In general, the equity share of an investment project would be 30–35 percent, with debt financing covering the balance. Large state-owned port enterprises possessing project approval documents from the central government need not provide collateral, widening access to debt markets. An illustration of the revenue streams for port enterprises is shown in figure 2.7.

Port tariffs

The funding of port investments has been closely related to how port tariffs are set and regulated and how tariff revenues are allocated. Port tariffs have long been an instrument of international trade, balanced by a need to ensure that revenues are sufficient to cover operating costs and, depending on how ports are financed, to contribute to recovery of investment costs. Although there is now broad acceptance that port tariffs should at least cover operating costs, there is less agreement on the extent to which they should help recover investment costs. This lack of agreement on recovery of investment costs allows governments to use port tariffs as instruments of macroeconomic strategy.

Illustration of revenue sources for port enterprises

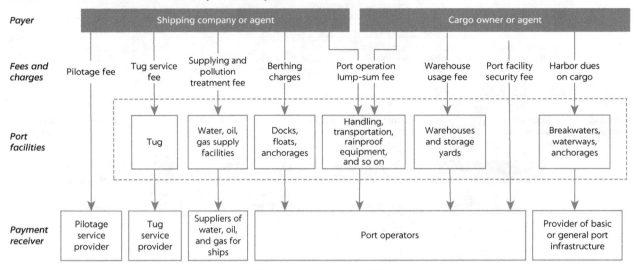

Source: Original analysis conducted for this report by PricewaterhouseCoopers (PwC).

At the outset of China's opening to the world, the government (through the Ministry of Communications) cited macroeconomic strategy as the justification for setting port charges at certain levels. As foreign investment in and operation of ports became more prevalent, especially in the operation of container terminals, government control over port tariffs was relaxed somewhat. As decentralization progressed, local governments adjusted port charges to optimize cost recovery and price competitiveness, eyeing the practices of other ports.

Since 2015, the MoT has continued to promote the market-oriented reform of port charges and merged redundant items to form a simplified list of charges. According to "Port Charges and Charges Measures" port charges are now categorized as (1) government-determined, (2) government-guided, or (3) enterprise-determined (Ministry of Transport and National Development and Reform Commission 2015).

In 2019, a notice on the revision of port charges reduced some government charges (including cargo port charges, security fees, and pilotage fees), consolidated certain charges, and required pricing policies to be enforced and regulated (Ministry of Transport and National Development and Reform Commission 2019). Most important in the first category are port construction fees; designed as a dedicated source of funding for coastal public port facilities, IWT infrastructure and inland ports are now used as a tool for macroeconomic policy (box 2.4).

In 2020, the port construction fee was removed, and the fee to compensate for ship pollution was cut in half. The same year, all government-determined port charges were reduced by 20 percent from March 1 to June 30 as a way to stimulate trade following the initial downturn at the start of the COVID-19 (coronavirus) pandemic. These fee modifications were later extended to the end of 2020.

BOX 2.4

Port construction fees

Port construction fees were introduced in October 1985 (Measures for the Collection of Port Construction Fees) and implemented in 1986 (State Council 1985b). The fees were levied on goods entering and leaving 26 Chinese ports,[a] including all imports and exports as well as domestic trade between the ports. The fees were charged only once per voyage. For instance, imported goods from other countries were generally subject to port construction fees at their destination port, not other ports of transit. These fees were paid by the goods' consignor or consignee, collected by the local port authorities, and transferred to the Ministry of Transport (MoT) (Ministry of Communications 1985).

Port construction fees became an important funding source for the MoT, with ¥ 2 billion (approximately US$580 million) collected in 1986. Their level has been changed and updated several times to meet the funding needs of port construction projects. In 1993, the central government and other ministries issued a notice on expanding the range of the fees, raising rates, and levying surcharges for waterborne passengers and freight (State Council, Ministry of Finance, Ministry of Transport, and Price Bureau 1993). The policy stated that the collection of fees would be extended to all ports involved in international trade; the fees collected would be used specifically for container infrastructure construction. Additional rules and measures for the collection of fees, including collection methods, were issued in the same year.

Although the addition of rules and changes in pricing were meant to ensure the accurate and standardized collection of fees across all ports, the total amount of port construction fees collected in 2000 was about the same as it had been in 1986, even though port throughput had tripled.

In addition, the rationale behind fee collection became difficult to justify as terminal ownership and use changed over time. Specifically, the port facilities built and financed by cargo owners and inland provinces, as explained previously, had received no investment from the MoT. The users of these terminals saw it as unfair that they were charged in the same manner as those who used MoT-funded terminals. In 2011, the MoT established new rates, lowering fees for every category by 20 percent as compared with 1993 rates. In 2016, regulations on port charges were promulgated by the MoT and the National Development and Reform Commission (Ministry of Transport and National Development and Reform Commission 2015). The regulation covered the assessment of cargo port charges, security fees for port facilities, port operation fees for passenger ships, pilotage fees, and berthing fees, among others. Its purpose was to clarify and standardize port import and export charges, promote market-oriented port service charges, and simplify previous fee structures. The regulation also explicitly states which prices are to be set by the government and which by the market.

a. These were the ports of Basuo, Beihai, Dalian, Fangcheng, Fuzhou, Guangzhou, Haikou, Huangpu, Lianyungang, Nanjing, Nantong, Ningbo, Qingdao, Qinhuangdao, Sanya, Shanghai, Shantou, Shijiu, Tianjin, Wenzhou, Xiamen, Yantai, Yingkou, Zhangjiagang, Zhanjiang, and Zhenjiang.

Foreign investment and joint ventures

The use of foreign investment to finance greenfield port projects in China has undergone several reforms. In 1985, recognizing that port construction projects were capital intensive, time consuming, and likely to yield a low rate of return, the State Council (1985a) issued interim regulations on preferential treatment for Sino-foreign joint ventures in harbor and wharf construction.

This milestone marked a turnaround in the central government's attitude toward foreign investment in the port industry. An initial ban on foreign investment was replaced by active encouragement of the involvement of foreign companies in joint ventures. Such joint ventures would not only provide the funds needed to finance the construction of port projects, but would also introduce technology and management know-how to the industry (Roehrig 1994). The provisions stated that foreign companies could jointly invest in the construction of terminals with contract lengths of more than 30 years. Moreover, foreign companies could be exempted from customs duties and commercial and industrial taxes, as well as income taxes, for five years once the terminals became profitable. For the following five years, taxes would be reduced by half. These preferential terms could also be extended in certain cases, and programs with relatively low investment returns could also be supplemented with profits from programs with higher yields.

After these provisions were issued, the Nanjing Port Authority and the American Encinal Terminals formed the first Sino-foreign joint venture in China's port sector, the Nanjing International Container Terminal Handling Co. Ltd.

Despite these changes, restrictions remained on foreign companies. Joint ventures with a domestic company were at that time the only mechanism by which foreign entities could enter the Chinese maritime market, and their main operational bases had to be in China. Moreover, foreign investors could hold no more than a 49 percent stake in any Chinese terminal (Cullinane and Wang 2006; National Bureau of Statistics of China 2004–19).

In 1992, measures were taken to increase foreign investment in different parts of China's port sector. The MoT released regulations on expanding and accelerating transportation development through deeper reforms (Ministry of Transport 1992). One purpose was to allow foreign investors to build dedicated docks and waterways for cargo owners. In addition, joint ventures were allowed to undertake cargo operations and domestic freight transportation, own infrastructure for terminal operations, and lease wharves.

The measures taken in 1992 opened more opportunities. The Port of Shanghai and the Hutchison Whampoa group (Hong Kong SAR, China) launched a joint venture; in south China, the Port of Shenzhen also formed a joint venture with Hutchison Whampoa for the development of the Yantian port area. Eventually, other transnational operators, such as Singapore's PSA and Denmark's AP Møller, formed joint ventures with Chinese firms.

The advantages of joint ventures, particularly at this point in the reform process, were fourfold. First, these world-leading transnational operators brought with them advanced equipment and management skills that Chinese seaports needed to close the gap with modern maritime transport systems. Their operations became showcases advancing the learning of their Chinese counterparts.

Second, these operators were either self-financed or had loans from the international capital market, which helped to ease the problem of inadequate funding. Third, they brought with them shipping clients, allowing Chinese ports to establish shipping services to major market destinations earlier than might otherwise have been the case. Some shipping lines became shareholders in container terminals themselves, showing confidence in the future of China's port industry. Finally, as business entities, the joint ventures challenged the Chinese port authorities, eventually impelling them to transform ports into marketplaces governed by international standards.

Starting in 1995, the "Catalogue for the Guidance of Foreign Investment Industries," compiled and updated by various departments of the central

FIGURE 2.8
Potential forms of entry for foreign companies in China's port sector

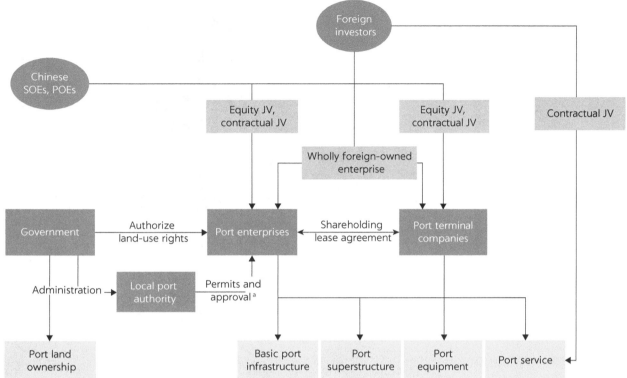

Source: Original analysis conducted for this report by PricewaterhouseCoopers (PwC).
Note: JV = joint venture; POE = privately owned enterprise; SOE = state-owned enterprise.
a. Ministry of Transport is responsible for approvals for building terminals with the capacity to handle 10,000 or greater deadweight-ton vessels.

government, encouraged foreign investment in the design and manufacture of port machinery, as well as the construction and operation of public port terminals, though the Chinese partners still had to hold a majority stake in any joint ventures (SPC, SETC, and MoFTEC 1995). In 2002, a revised catalogue removed the limits on foreign equity ownership of public port terminals and gave foreign investors the power to set their own prices for cargo handling fees, increasing their enthusiasm for China (SPC, SETC, and MoFTEC 2002).

As it was in the area of governance, the Port Law of 2004 was the first Chinese law to specifically regulate port investment and financing, thereby providing legal protection to both domestic and foreign companies investing in port development and operations. The law removed entry barriers for both Chinese and foreign investors, as well as the 49 percent limitation initially imposed on the foreign investors. Any qualified group, whether domestic or foreign, could now apply to invest in port development and operations. The ruling significantly opened Chinese ports to foreign capital as an important driver of port capacity.

The conditions under which foreign investors can invest in Chinese ports have evolved. Figure 2.8 illustrates the three different potential forms of entry for foreign companies. Figure 2.9 shows the evolution of foreign direct investment in Chinese ports.

FIGURE 2.9

Foreign direct investment in China's ports, 1991–2019

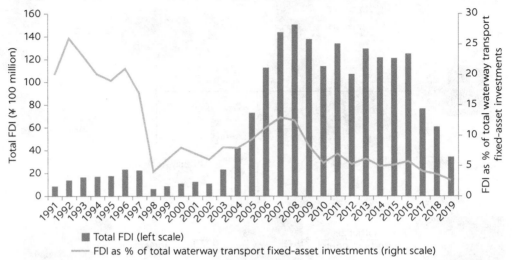

Total FDI (left scale)

FDI as % of total waterway transport fixed-asset investments (right scale)

Source: National Bureau of Statistics of China 2004–19.
Note: FDI = foreign direct investment.

PLANNING AND DEVELOPMENT OF PORTS AND PORT CITIES

Two major reforms in the 1980s changed the dynamics of port-city relationships in China. First, in 1984, the central government designated 14 port cities as "coastal open cities" and exempted them from provincial taxes. Two more port cities, Yingkou and Weihai, were added to the list in 1985 and 1988, respectively (Cao 2001).

As the economy grew, ports also expanded, not just in trade volumes but also in physical size. In addition, they attracted other industries and logistics operations, particularly those using the port to import raw materials or export products.

As port throughput increases, the city population typically grows as well. China's four port megacities—Guangzhou, Shanghai, Shenzhen, and Tianjin—have witnessed major growth in both port throughput and population. Among them, three have absorbed nearby jurisdictions to create new districts in which port activities can be carried out—Pudong New District in Shanghai, Nansha New District in Guangzhou, and Binhai New District in Tianjin. Shenzhen is a special case: it has two port areas, Yantian to the east and Shekou to the west of Hong Kong SAR, China. The city has no new district to expand into, which has led future growth of port activities to the Port of Nansha in Guangzhou, leading to port regionalization among port cities in the Pearl River Delta.

Other than in the top four mega port cities, the population size of other cities has not grown with their port throughput beyond a certain scale. As shown in figure 2.10, population scales are stabilized at two levels: 5–10 million, as in Ningbo, Dalian, and Qingdao; and less than 3 million, as in Rizhao and Yingkou. The latter category of port city still looks very large by international comparison, although they are regarded as third- or fourth-tier cities in China.

Figure 2.11 illustrates the relationship between port throughput and GDP in 15 port cities from 1980 to 2015. The port cities can be divided into three categories: (1) cities with rapid growth in both throughput volume and GDP, such as Shanghai,

FIGURE 2.10

Relationship between population size and port throughput in several Chinese port cities

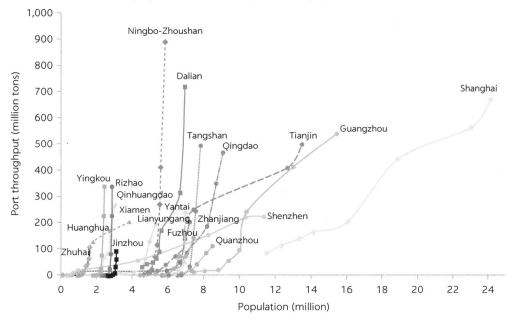

Source: Wang 2020.
Note: Dots represent sampling years.

FIGURE 2.11

Relationship between port throughput and GDP in several Chinese port cities, 1980–2015

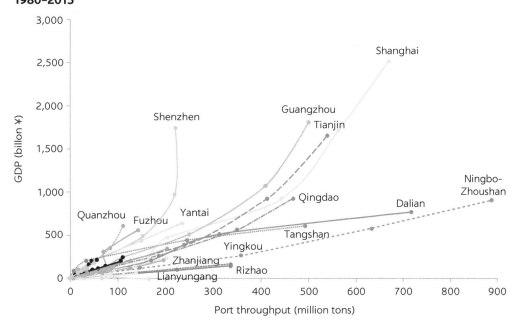

Source: Wang 2020.
Note: Dots represent sampling years. ¥ = yuan.

Guangzhou, Tianjin, and Qingdao; (2) cities with rapid growth in throughput and steady but moderate growth in GDP, such as Ningbo, Dalian, Tangshan, Yingkou, Lianyungang, Rizhao, and Zhanjiang; and (3) cities with rapid GDP growth but moderate or stable port throughput, such as Shenzhen.

To understand the causal impact of ports on the economic outcomes of port cities, a rigorous econometric analysis was conducted that exploited a planning policy shock on China's ports in 2006. The findings show that cities with major ports have attracted large amounts of foreign direct investment and have relatively high levels of GDP per capita when compared with cities without a port. The classification of ports into main ports, major ports, and supporting ports by the MoT allows for an analysis of the effects of this classification on the economic development of the port city. Major ports were given more funding for upgrades, and it is significant that these port upgrades, which increased the throughput of the targeted ports, led to higher fixed-asset investments and foreign direct investment in the cities hosting these ports, as well as higher GDP per capita. In addition, port cities perform better on all three outcomes as compared with neighboring cities that do not have ports.

In line with the positive effect of ports on the regional economy, port cities have embraced port development as an engine for economic growth (box 2.5). Favorable tax policies and subsidies for ports have been issued over time by local governments. For instance, land for a port's wharves is often exempted from land-use taxes (State Administration of Taxation 1989). In line with the central government's Land Administration Law, land used for transportation infrastructure supported by the state may be and often is provided free of charge (State Council 2004a). Cities also support port development through land exchanges. Ports relocate away from the city center for a variety of reasons, including limited space and lack of water depth for ships. Depending on the trajectory of city growth, such a move can also be beneficial for the city. Relocating a port away from the city center can reduce negative environmental and transportation impacts while freeing up space for urban waterfront development.

BOX 2.5

Ports as an anchor for growth: The case of the Binhai New Area

The Tianjin Binhai New Area is located on the east coast of Tianjin, about 120 kilometers from Beijing, and is part of the Bohai Economic Rim. The area, which includes the Port of Tianjin, was formally approved in 2009 under the 11th Five-Year Plan (2006–10). Envisioned as a gateway from northern China to the rest of the world, its nine functional zones include a port area, an international shipping and logistics center, high-tech industries, heavy chemical industries, tourism, and service industries.

Since 2008, the Tianjin municipal government has been supporting the opening of the Binhai New Area through policy reform and financial support. Part of the Tianjin municipal government's special fund has been used to enhance the capacity of the Dongjiang Free Trade Port Zone, with the aim of attracting companies dealing with shipping logistics, import-export processing, warehousing, specialized transport, procurement and distribution, and other shipping-related activities. To that end, such companies were given discounts on the purchase or lease of office buildings and space in the Dongjiang Free Trade Port Zone. Small and medium-size enterprises were also granted subsidized loans on advantageous terms.

Source: Song, Wu, and Xu 2019.

Land-use planning is important in port cities, especially where large shares of urban land are being taken for port activities. As cities grow, alternative land uses can emerge, leading to disputes over the amount of urban land that should be used for port functions. To mitigate negative land-use impacts, local governments and port enterprises in China work together so that the land is allocated to its most productive use. In situations in which port-related industries and services have expanded before large-scale urban development has taken place, key sites are often taken up by these industries in an unproductive manner. Space in the city center used for factories might be better used for commercial, office, or residential purposes. In this situation, relocation of these functions is negotiated and implemented with policy support from city governments.

For example, the proportion of industrial land in Dalian's main urban area used to be relatively high, at about 21.4 percent. Since 2004, an industrial zone adjacent to the port and away from the city center has been built. Not only did the municipal government provide financial support for construction, but it also enacted policies to encourage industries to move into the industrial park, such as tax incentives and streamlined procedures that can save time and money at customs (Livermore 2007). Some 205 enterprises relocated to the industrial zone, freeing up more than 6.6 square kilometers of land in the city. About 40 percent of this land has been used for the construction of public facilities such as highways, public squares, parks, and green spaces, while the rest has been used for residential apartments and commercial buildings. What was once a heavy-chemicals industrial city has now been transformed into a city for residents, white-collar businesses, culture, and tourism. Shenzhen and Shanghai offer additional examples of how a port can anchor urban growth (boxes 2.6 and 2.7).

BOX 2.6

A model for the development of port cities: The case of Shenzhen

Shenzhen Industrial Zone, located in Shenzhen across the bay from Hong Kong SAR, China, has become a model for the development of port cities in China. Until China Merchants Group was given the rights to develop the area into Shekou Industrial Zone in 1979, it was no more than a customs office in Bao'an County. Development was initially focused on Shekou Port, which opened in early 1981. China Merchants Shekou Industrial Zone Holdings (CMSK), a subsidiary of China Merchants Group, relied mainly on special policies and the area's geographical proximity to Hong Kong SAR, China, to vigorously develop import- and export-processing industries. Local officials provided trade incentives and a user-friendly investment policy, while rapidly building the necessary infrastructure to sustain industry (Grogan 2019). As the Chinese economy grew, Shenzhen entered a new phase: formation of the industrial park. In 1995, Shenzhen redoubled its efforts to strengthen industrial operations, while expanding infrastructure and supporting services. During this period, the simple processing and manufacturing activities in the park started to shift to medium- and high-end industries. Eventually, these industries were replaced by high-tech enterprises, and the focus of companies in the industrial zone shifted to financial, venture capital, and trade services. In addition to the industrial aspects of the city, after 2001 CMSK began to focus on urban development, transforming the city from a living area for employees of the port and industrial park to an attractive, modern, coastal city. High-quality housing and services were offered to residents, and it also become a tourism

continued

center, combining entertainment with high-end tourism real estate (CMSK, n.d.). The new city generates income streams that are no longer port related. Today Shenzhen's per capita GDP is greater than US$30,000.

The Shenzhen port-city model has been named "front-port, central-park, back-city" (前港-中区-后城). Since 2017, China Merchants Group has been promoting global replication of this model. It is building specialized industrial new towns in several cities in China,[a] and has been exploring the possibility of exporting the model overseas under the Belt and Road Initiative to countries such as Djibouti, Sri Lanka, Tanzania, and Togo.

Although the model has its benefits, it should be noted that the initial development of Shenzhen relied heavily on the existence of Hong Kong SAR, China, in particular the sophisticated logistics services associated with the Port of Hong Kong, at that time one of the world's largest. In addition, advocates of the Shenzhen model tend to emphasize the property development gains of the "back-city" component of the model, which were also driven to a large extent by the high cost of land in Hong Kong SAR, China. The exceptionally fast growth of Shenzhen has therefore been due to a unique set of circumstances that may be difficult to replicate elsewhere.

a. In 2018, China Merchants Group and Zhanjiang City announced they were cooperating to build a "Beibu Gulf-Shekou" in accordance with this comprehensive new development model.

BOX 2.7

Complexity in port development beyond the city border: The case of Shanghai

Shanghai is one of the oldest ports in China. Its general cargo wharves were built a century ago along the Huangpu River, today the city center (map B2.7.1). When the port began to modernize by adding container terminals in the 1980s, these terminals first stretched from the city center to Zhanghuabang near Wusongkou, where the Huangpu meets the Yangtze. To accommodate much larger vessels, the Waigaoqiao area in Pudong New District along the Yangtze became the first port relocation in Shanghai. The terminals were to have a 13-meter draft, the deepest in its jurisdiction. The project came with land to be turned into a new industrial cluster and large-scale urban expansion. Since then, most of the riverside of the Huangpu River has been redeveloped into an eye-catching waterfront put to multiple urban uses.

But by the time Waigaoqiao was completed in 2000, Shanghai had already found it inadequate to meet the national government's wish for a regional hub that could serve as the core of the future Shanghai International Shipping Center, a regional port system serving the entire Yangtze River Delta. The problem was that the water was not deep enough to accommodate the oceangoing vessels used by major shipping lines. Therefore, it became imperative to build container terminals near Shanghai with a draft of at least 18 meters. Yangshan Port was then built as part of the Port of Shanghai but located on Lesser Yangshan Island (in the municipality of Zhoushan, Zhejiang province), some 100 kilometers from the Shanghai city center.

The Yangshan container terminals began operation in December 2005, and some international

continued

Box 2.7, *continued*

MAP B2.7.1

The relocation of the Port of Shanghai to Zhanghuabang, Waigaoqiao, and Yangshan

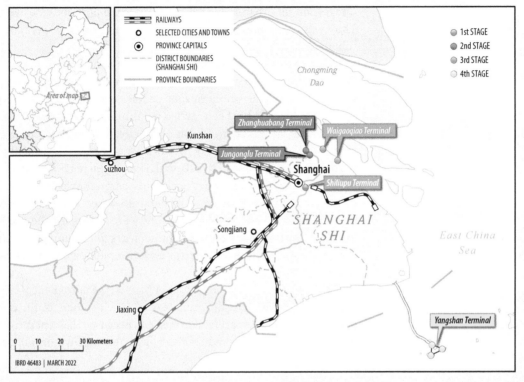

Source: World Bank, based on data from the China Waterborne Transport Research Institute (WTI).

shipping routes to and from Shanghai moved there. The expansion and relocation of international container shipping to the island were complicated for at least three reasons. The first was the coordination required between Shanghai and the host city of Zhoushan, which would not have been possible without the support and leadership of the Ministry of Transport. The most difficult sticking points were the arrangements between the two governments for splitting the profits and tax revenues generated by the port, and the relocation and compensation of residents on Lesser Yangshan. The second complication was the building of the Donghai Bridge, 33 kilometers in length, the first of its kind in China. Third and most important was the free-port status (bonded trade zone) granted by the State Council to both Yangshan Port on the island and its logistics park on the mainland side of Donghai Bridge. This southernmost area

of Shanghai was renamed Lingang ("near the port") New City, and the bonded trade zone soon benefited from favorable policies and regulations that facilitated the trade and e-commerce of imported consumer goods.

After 15 years of effort, Lingang New City now enjoys not only the presence of major logistics service providers, such as Prologis and Schenker, residing inside the international trade park, but also a large group of automobile firms clustered nearby, including the first and largest Tesla plant outside the United States. The 14th Five-Year Plan (2021–25) calls for Lingang New City to grow to 295 square kilometers by 2035, much larger than the other four new cities in the suburbs of Shanghai. The projected expansion partly reflects the planned relocation of industries to this area, which should lessen the traffic and emissions problems found in Pudong.

Ports generally have a positive economic impact. However, they are also associated with negative effects, notably sharp rises in urban congestion as hinterland traffic flows to and from the port. The high percentage of freight flows in China using trucks contributes to urban congestion as well as to traffic accidents and delays. Traffic problems stem not just from freight traffic, but also from people commuting to work in the port or related industries. Congestion on urban roads can, in turn, make port activities less efficient. Thus, urban transport planning has been a major focus for port cities in China (photo 2.1).

China has sought to mitigate the negative transportation impacts of ports on its cities in several ways. The first is by increasing the proportion of freight using rail and inland water transport, while decreasing the role of road transport. This objective has been carried out through several measures, including new railway infrastructure, a rail-connected dry port system, and improvements to the inland waterway network. At present, only a small percentage of container freight moves by rail, with few coastal ports having on-dock container rail yards; but in most ports bulk cargo moves by rail (photo 2.2). Although there have been some modal shifts away from road transportation, much remains to be done. In addition to incentives for the use of rail and inland water transport, there are other ways to discourage the use of road transportation, such as toll systems and the enforcement of weight limits on trucks.

Cities can also impose surcharges or bans on the movement of trucks during peak hours, either citywide or in areas of the city where traffic congestion is particularly bad (a less preferable measure because it has a negative impact on port productivity). China has also sought to improve urban transport by

PHOTO 2.1

Qingdao city and port

Source: © VCG. Used with the permission of VCG. Further permission required for reuse.

Rail-port connectivity, Qinhuangdao Port

attempting to separate port traffic from urban traffic. For example, the layout of industrial zones can be planned to reduce interference between port and industrial traffic and general urban traffic. The development of Tianjin has been based on a unified plan to reduce spatial conflicts between these two types of traffic. There are strictly controlled reserve lands between the Binhai New Area and the industrial zones, which should help prevent spatial conflicts in the future. Building new infrastructure specifically for port traffic is another method that has been used. In Tianjin, the main urban area of Tanggu is close to the back of the port, so port traffic inevitably crosses the urban area. The solution used here has been to build an elevated highway behind the port to which port roads are directly linked, eliminating the need for port traffic to enter Tanggu.

HINTERLAND TRANSPORT POLICIES AND CONNECTIVITY

Figure 2.12 shows freight volumes for road, rail, and inland waterway transport between 1978 and 2018. Road infrastructure grew more than other inland transport options between 1978 and 2018. The construction of expressways has been a significant driver in this respect: these tolled high-capacity, high-speed, multi-lane roadways have reduced road transport times and costs. The Shanghai-Jiading Expressway was the first to open, in 1988, closely followed by the Shenyang-Dalian Expressway in northeastern China.

Road

Expressways grew slowly at first, but after 1998, between 3,000 and 10,000 kilometers of new expressways were opened each year. In December 2004, the

FIGURE 2.12

Volume of freight moved by roads, inland waterways, and railways in China, 1978–2018

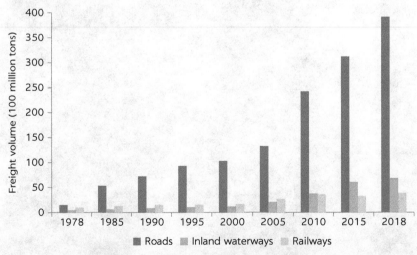

Source: China Waterborne Transport Research Institute (WTI).
Note: This figure shows total freight by each mode, not just to and from ports. However, the trends are believed to be indicative of port traffic by mode. Also, the data relate to tons, whereas data relating to ton-kilometers would be more indicative of the total transport task, given that road transport involves much more short-distance trade than do the other modes.

State Council (2004a) approved a plan for the National Trunk Highway System, which aimed to build an expressway network of 85,000 kilometers over three decades, connecting all provincial capitals and cities with more than 200,000 residents. The target was exceeded in less than eight years, partly because of growing demand stemming from the liberalization of road haulage in 2005.

Expressway planning is a function of the MoT, but most of China's expressways are owned by commercial corporations. These corporations have varying degrees of public and private ownership and can borrow money from banks or securities markets based on projected toll revenues. After completing the construction of a toll expressway, provincial governments often establish an expressway corporation as a public limited company listed on the stock exchange, reinvesting the proceeds in more toll road construction. Public-private partnerships have also been used for expressway construction. For example, the Guangzhou-Shenzhen-Zhuhai Expressway (opened in 1999 under a 30-year concession) is an early pilot of a build-operate-transfer scheme. By 2018, China had more than 140,000 kilometers of expressways.

Rail

Flexibility in ownership and financing allowed China to expand its expressway network quickly, particularly when compared with the rail network, which is financed to a larger extent with public grants. The rail network has expanded over the past 40 years, but more slowly than road infrastructure. Significant quality improvements have been made. For example, the proportion of total route length that is double-tracked rose from 24 percent in 1990 to 58 percent in 2018; the proportion that is electrified rose from 12 percent to 70 percent. Although China is well-suited to rail freight, with large flows of bulk goods moving over long distances, its rail network at the start of the reform period was small by international standards, whether measured in relation to land area or population. China's rail network has more than doubled in size since 1978, but it remains small when compared with those of other large countries.

The immediate response to capacity constraints in the early 2000s was to prioritize train movements, with passengers and military traffic taking precedence, and bulk cargo such as coal and grain coming next (photo 2.3). Shortages of rail capacity and a low position in the pecking order are among the reasons why the use of rail for long-distance container traffic from ports has been so slow to take off. In 2003, the Ministry of Railways prepared the Mid- and Long-Term Railway Network Plan (Ministry of Railways 2003) to identify investment needs through 2020. The plan called for the total operational length of the rail network to increase by one-third, to 100,000 kilometers, with separate high-speed dedicated passenger lines and freight routes on the main corridors and 50 percent of the rail network either double-tracked or electrified or both. The plan also included high-capacity coal transport corridors, the development of container transport, and schemes for strengthening the network in the west. Less attention was paid to the need to increase axle loads and train lengths for freight, although the intention was set to lengthen routes capable of carrying double-stack container trains from to 1,460 kilometers in 2005 (the Shanghai-Beijing route) to 16,460 kilometers by 2020.

Overall, the proportion of containers moved by rail from coastal ports has remained low, at only 1.7 percent of total port container throughput (see table 1.8

in chapter 1). The top 10 ports for rail-sea container shipments in 2018 moved, on average, about 3 percent of their total port container throughput by rail.

A large part of the network expansion was to be in the form of high-speed passenger lines, which were expected to free up space for freight on conventional lines (Lawrence, Bullock, and Liu 2019). However, demand for conventional trains has remained higher than expected, limiting the desired increase in capacity for freight. As a result, in mid-2016, the National Development and Reform Commission released the latest five-year update to the development plan for China's railways, revising its target upward to 175,000 route-kilometers by 2025.

Most rail investment in China has been undertaken by the central government, but since the early 1990s the sector has slowly opened to new participants through joint ventures for rail development. Indeed, since 2008, all new and upgraded lines have been financed on a joint-venture basis. The impetus has been the continued lack of network capacity and the scale of the funding required to expand it. Joint ventures have generally been built and operated more efficiently and competitively than similar state-owned rail lines.

The first policy document encouraging joint ventures was issued in 1992; regulations governing their development were in place by 1996. As a result, the number of joint-venture railways increased from 22 in 1995 (4.4 percent of total network length) to 170 by 2013 (39.6 percent of total length). The length of the networks in both years is specified in table 2.3.

As well as operating on their own tracks, joint-venture rail companies are also allowed to operate using the national network if sufficient capacity is available. For example, the Baoshen Railway Corporation has been able to run five coal trains per day on the national network from Shenmu (Shanxi province) to Qinhuangdao Port (box 2.8).

PHOTO 2.3
Bulk terminal, Port of Yantai

Source: © VCG. Used with the permission of VCG. Further permission required for reuse.

TABLE 2.3 **Length of national and joint-venture railways in China, 1995 and 2013**

YEAR	LENGTH OF CENTRAL GOVERNMENT-OWNED RAILWAYS (KILOMETERS)	LENGTH OF JOINT VENTURE-OWNED RAILWAYS (KILOMETERS)
1995	54,616	2,738
2013	67,212	47,852

Source: National Bureau of Statistics of China 2019.

BOX 2.8

Joint ventures linked to ports: The success of Daqin Railways

Daqin Railways is a dedicated coal line running east-west in northern China. It connects Datong, a coal mining center in Shanxi province, to Qinhuangdao Port. Construction of the railway started in 1985, and operations began in 1992. An expansion of the railway line begun in 2003 and completed in 2010 added 600 million tons of carrying capacity. In 2006, the railway was listed on the Shanghai Stock Exchange.

The Daqin line is dedicated entirely to coal traffic, and more than 90 percent of the coal moving through

Qinhuangdao Port is transported along it. In 2018, the Daqin line transported 440 million tons of freight, making it the world's busiest freight railway.

Shenmu-Huanghua Railway is another line nearly parallel to the Daqin line (map B2.8.1); it links another important coal mining region with the Port of Huanghua. Both Qinhuangdao Port and the Port of Huanghua are critical hubs in China's coal logistics system.

MAP B2.8.1

Daqin line linking Datong to Qinhuangdao Port

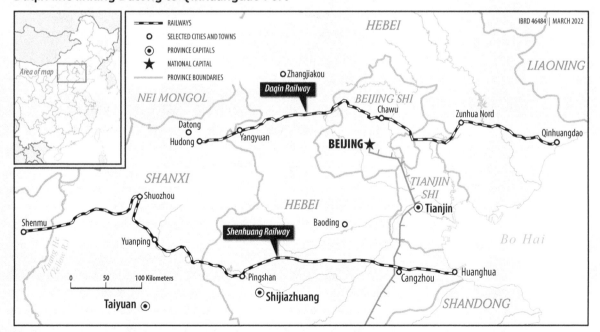

Source: World Bank, based on data from the China Waterborne Transport Research Institute (WTI).

Ports have always been of great interest to joint-venture railway companies because of their role in consolidating traffic. Many bulk terminals are owned by a single user or a small group of companies, importing or exporting based on long-term contracts, with stockpiles at the port or mine to even out peaks in demand and supply. The large, predictable cargo flows that result make it relatively easy to raise finances for investment.

Even with the use of joint ventures, however, the shortage of capacity for rail freight has remained. In 2014, the government set up a new railway development fund to attract private investment into the sector. The China Railway Development Fund is scheduled to operate for 15 to 20 years, with an option to extend if approved by the State Council. Preferred stockholders will receive a fixed return on investment but will not participate in the management of the fund, 70 percent of which will be earmarked for railway projects approved by the State Council, while the remaining 30 percent can be invested in other projects, such as land development. In its first round of fundraising in June 2014, the Railway Development Fund raised ¥ 8.2 billion (US$1.27 billion), much of it from three of China's big four state-owned banks, as well as the Industrial Bank based in Fujian province.

Inland waterways

China has also undertaken a gradual market opening in inland water transport. Economic development and environmental imperatives placed this mode of transport high on the national agenda. An important milestone was the approval in 2007 of the Layout Plan of National Inland Waterways and Ports by the State Council (Ministry of Transport 2007b). This plan laid out the strategic vision for China's inland waterway network under the umbrella of the 2-1-2-18 Network (map 2.4) (Aritua et al. 2020).

The network has the following components:

- Two horizontal routes: the Yangtze River and the Pearl River trunk waterways
- One vertical route: the Grand Canal
- Two networks: the Yangtze River Delta and the Pearl River Delta
- Eighteen high-grade waterways and their tributaries: ten tributaries of the Yangtze River Basin; three tributaries of the Pearl River Basin; and the Huai, Shaying, Heilong, Songhua, and Min Rivers.

The coordinated efforts of the central government—coupled with the clear roles and responsibilities of the various institutions involved, robust funding, and dedicated educational institutions—have translated into soaring investments and volumes (figure 2.13).

Between 2002 and 2016, China's inland water transport system was the most heavily used in the world. As of 2018, the length of the navigable national inland waterway network was 127,126 kilometers, according to the MoT. About 52 percent of it can accommodate only the smallest commercial vessels. Larger vessels (more than 1,000 tons of capacity) can use only 10 percent of the navigable waterways.

The Yangtze River system, including its trunk line and tributaries, is the longest and most used segment of the network (see table 1.7 in chapter 1). It also boasts the largest inland ports as measured by throughput. After the Yangtze, the

IBRD 45269 |
AUGUST 2020

MAP 2.4

The 2-1-2-18 Inland Waterway Network in China

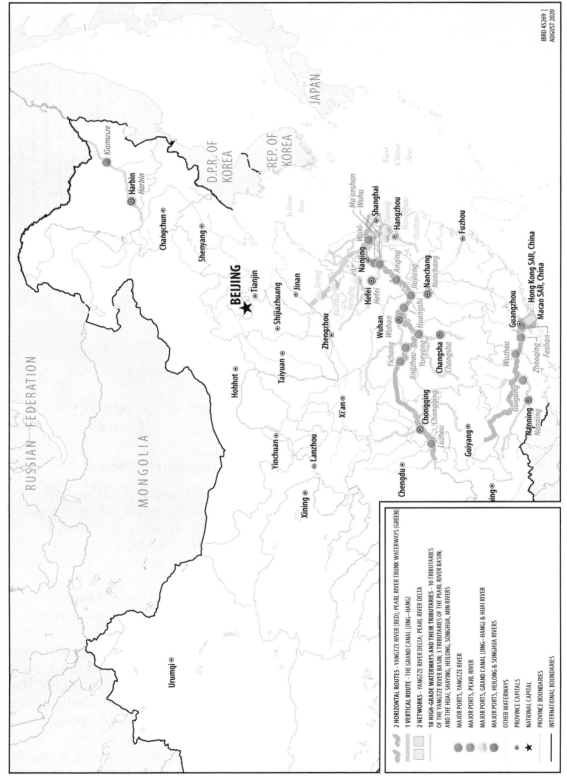

FIGURE 2.13

Investments in inland waterways and volumes handled at inland ports in China, 1978–2018

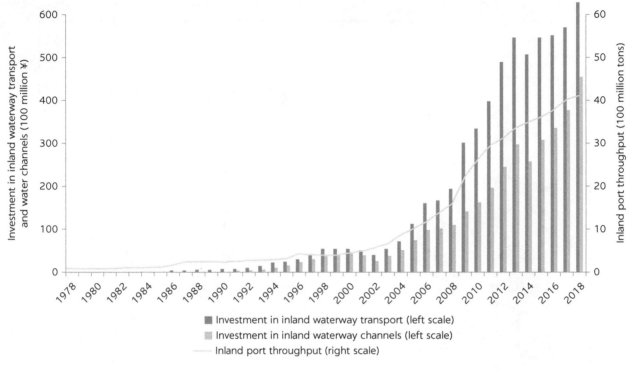

Source: Ministry of Transport 2019.
Note: ¥ = yuan.

Pearl River is the second-most used for cargo transport. The Pearl and Huai Rivers together account for about a quarter of the navigable waterways.

The modal split of freight transport in China

Roads' share of total cargo transported rose from 50 percent in 1978 to 79 percent in 2018, almost entirely at the expense of rail (figure 2.14). In 1978–85, road transport accounted for almost all traffic growth, taking market share away from both rail and inland waterways. In 1985–2000, the market shares of all three modes of transport remained stable. Between 2005 and 2017, rail lost market share, mainly to inland waterways.

The declining share of rail is at least partly because of the drop in coal demand within China, given government efforts to reduce pollution in the eastern provinces. Moreover, Chinese railways were too slow to take advantage of the opportunity presented by the growing demand for long-distance container transport. This was partly due to a failure to develop sufficient on-dock rail terminals in the major Chinese ports, on the one hand, and low uptake of opportunities to use multiple modes, on the other. The Chinese rail network has also experienced serious capacity constraints, with priority given mainly to passenger traffic. Meanwhile, tariff regulations promulgated by the National Development and Reform Commission have made it nearly impossible for the railway sector to match the tariffs offered by competing road transport firms. Although many trucking companies pay highway tolls, which are said to account for up to 30 percent of their operating costs in some cases, railway tariffs include freight surcharges imposed over and above basic charges to provide capital for

FIGURE 2.14

Chinese freight traffic, by mode of transport, 1978–2018

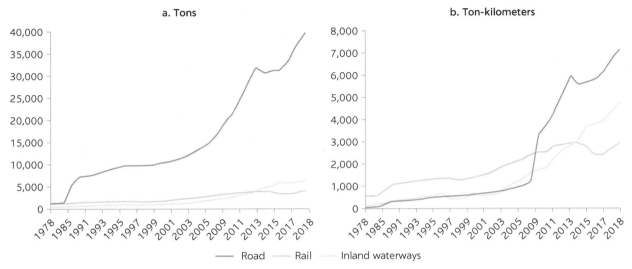

Source: China Statistical Yearbook.

new lines and infrastructure upgrades through a dedicated railway construction fund. Although it is true that the railways in China do not suffer from such a large infrastructure cost disadvantage as railways in many other countries (where highways are provided free of charge, but rail traffic must pay for its track costs), road transport is still able to compete with rail for certain types of cargo and over distances as great as 800 kilometers.

There may be some revival of rail transport in the future, given that shifting freight away from roads is a key priority of the 14th Five-Year Plan (2021–25) in efforts to tackle air pollution.[5] In 2017, the National Development and Reform Commission called for "deeper market reforms of rail freight prices, a complete and flexible freight pricing system, and the use of the market to allocate resources," to increase the proportion of freight moved by rail (National Development and Reform Commission 2017). But so far, reforms of the rail freight market appear to have had little effect.

Multimodalism

Multimodalism—the provision of door-to-door transport by more than one mode of transport under a single contract—has seen little progress up to now in China. One of the reasons has been China's tradition of centralized planning for each individual mode of transport, as evidenced by a long series of single-mode transportation plans, including the National Road Arteries Network Plan in 1981, the National Highway Network Plan in 2004, the National Road Network Plan (2013–30) in 2013, the Medium- and Long-Term Railway Network Plan of 2004 (updated in 2016), the National Coastal Port Layout Plan in 2006, and the National Inland Waterways and Port Layout Plan in 2007 (Ministry of Transport 2007b). However, the development of a comprehensive transportation network linking ports to the hinterlands via highways, railways, waterways, or even pipelines, requires integrated planning.

National plans set the goals for the country, which local governments customize to their own areas, striving to achieve consistency with national policies.

Governments at all levels, therefore, coordinate the development of each mode of transport through effective macro-control at the national level. Over time, the attention of national plans to the need for transport connectivity has increased. Between 2011 and 2019, for example, a number of policies were passed to promote multimodal transportation in China. These are included in appendix A.

However, obstacles to the growth of multimodal transport in China remain. First, although the MoT is now responsible for all interurban transport modes, coordination is poor among port hubs, railway hubs, inland waterway hubs, and dry ports, which for years were administered by different departments. Many container ports are not directly connected to the rail network, resulting in small proportions of rail-maritime multimodal transport. At present, rail-maritime multimodal transport in China accounts for only 2 percent of port container traffic. In addition, the number of freight hubs capable of carrying out multimodal operations remains low.

Second, despite government encouragement, the number of domestic enterprises that can offer multimodal transport remains low. Common difficulties include small corporate size or relatively backward outdated operating models, making it difficult to meet international multimodal service requirements.

Finally, China still lacks policies, laws, and regulations governing multimodal transport. Although regulations are in place for each of the different transport modes, a clear set of standardized regulations governing multimodal transport is still lacking. As such, the business environment is not yet suitable for full development of multimodalism.

Nevertheless, there have been some successes. Between 2010 and 2015, for example, container traffic moved by rail in six demonstration channels at the ports of Dalian, Lianyungang, Ningbo-Zhoushan, Qingdao, Shenzhen, and Tianjin increased from 1.41 million twenty-foot equivalent units (TEUs) to 2.37 million TEUs. Other projects include sea-rail transport of containers at ports along the Yangtze River, with the goal of demonstrating the advantages of multimodal transport.

Dry ports

The establishment of dry ports has made a major contribution to freight transport efficiency in China.[6] The basic functions of dry ports are shown in figure 2.15. A complete list of China's dry ports is provided in appendix B.

China's first dry port opened in Chaoyang, Beijing, in 2002. Preparations began in 1994 in an effort to improve trade connectivity and lower logistics costs (Beijing Customs and Tianjin Customs 1994). The Beijing Land Port International Logistics Co. Ltd. was then established in May 1999 to manage and operate the dry port in Chaoyang.

To raise the efficiency of interregional customs clearing, the General Administration of Customs established a cross-border rapid clearance model throughout China in 2001, enabling dry ports to be the designated destinations for freight coming in from abroad rather than needing another level of customs clearance between the Port of Tianjin and Chaoyang Inland Port. Then, in October 2002, Beijing and the Port of Tianjin signed their direct connection agreement, making Chaoyang the first dry port in China. It was designed to be a direct link between Beijing and the Port of Tianjin, and to serve the dual functions of being a customs supervision channel and a marine container transfer station. A milestone for the port came in March 2003, when the first batch of

FIGURE 2.15
Basic functions of inland dry ports

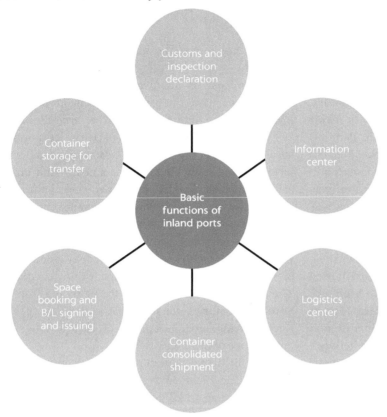

Source: China Waterborne Transport Research Institute (WTI).
Note: B/L = bill of lading.

imported "CIF (cost, insurance, and freight) Beijing" containers arrived at Chaoyang Inland Port, marking the fact that it had become a destination in its own right and a departure port for international maritime transport.

In August 2003, another milestone came when agents of shipping companies pre-approved by the national customs authorities were able to go through the formalities of container pickup using the manifest instead of the bill of lading. This model granted Chaoyang Inland Port true port status as recognized in the international shipping market.

At the start (2002–07) the development of dry ports was slow, with only 10 ports built and operated. After 2007, however, the development of dry ports accelerated rapidly, with many inland cities signing agreements with coastal ports. The spread of dry ports occurred from north to south, with the first being built in northeastern China by the Port of Dalian (box 2.9), the Port of Qingdao, and other ports around the Bohai Sea. Because coastal ports tended to start by building dry ports in the hinterland areas closest to them before expanding further inland, dry ports have also been expanding from east to west.

In addition to coastal ports, various players have taken the initiative to develop dry ports. The continuous increase in intraregional port competition has forced coastal ports to look for other business opportunities in their hinterlands

BOX 2.9

Cooperation between the Ports of Dalian and Shenyang

Shenyang, the capital city of Liaoning province, developed during World War II as a railway hub and industrial base for the manufacturing of military equipment. At the dawn of the twenty-first century, it was connected via six railway lines to major Chinese cities and to the Democratic People's Republic of Korea, Mongolia, and the Russian Federation. In 2003, the Port of Dalian invested in and converted part of Shenyang's eastern railway station into a dry port. Its initial land area was 13 hectares (later expanded to 23). The dry port was originally set up to provide transport and logistics solutions for the automobile industries of Shenyang. The two main clients were BMW Brilliance Automotive Ltd. (a joint venture between Brilliance Auto Group and BMW) and SAIC General Motors Corporation Ltd. (a joint venture between SAIC and General Motors). The existing rail service between Dayaowan (the Port of Dalian) and Shenyang's western railway station enjoyed a one-stop-shop at Shenyang West for customs declarations, inspections, and issuance and execution of bills of lading. The information systems for customs clearance and shipping schedules at the Port of Dalian are synchronized with those of the dry port. Shenyang's

dry port has joined the national Belt and Road Initiative.

The success of Shenyang's dry port can be attributed partly to the backing of its major client, BMW Brilliance Automotive Ltd. The carmaker has been a long-time client of the Port of Dalian; it exports automobile parts through the Dayaowan container terminals and assembled cars via a nearby roll-on, roll-off terminal. The five trains per week that run between Shenyang and the Port of Dalian carry mostly auto parts and have maintained shipments of at least 200,000 twenty-foot equivalent units (TEUs) per year since 2010, with the dry port capacity gradually increasing to 300,000 TEUs to meet this demand. The dry port now handles rail traffic to and from European countries, at a frequency of five trains per week, carrying automobile parts and other cargo from the province of Liaoning.

BMW Brilliance Automotive Ltd. recently constructed a new factory to produce automobiles in Dalian, less than 20 kilometers from the Dayaowan port area. This move creates a new challenge for the dry port in Shenyang, given that automobile manufacturing may shift to the new factory and cut demand for dry port services in Shenyang.

(box 2.10) (Abdoulkarim, Fatouma, and Munyao 2019). And because many ports have overlapping hinterlands, the independent or cooperative construction of inland dry ports has become an important way to strengthen competitiveness and gain a foothold in new markets.

In addition to port companies, inland cities have also invested in dry ports, either jointly with rail or port companies, or independently. Ganzhou, Nanchang, Xi'an, and Xingtai are examples of cities that have substantially reshaped the supply of local goods, energized logistics, and improved local economic development through the construction of dry ports.

In the market-based dry port development model, coastal ports and inland cities form strategic partnerships to build dry ports that will bring benefits to both parties. One of the major advantages of dry ports is their ability to provide efficient logistics, especially in customs clearance. The relevant ministries have issued various policies and legislation to reform China's logistics sector, including measures introduced by the General Administration of Customs that aim to simplify customs clearance procedures at dry ports for goods that must travel through different regions and jurisdictions (table 2.4). Under regional customs

BOX 2.10

The Port of Ningbo-Zhoushan

The Port of Ningbo-Zhoushan faces stiff competition from surrounding ports such as Shanghai, Xiamen, and Shenzhen, which all serve the Zhejiang and Jiangxi provinces. The Port of Shanghai has a geographical advantage over Ningbo-Zhoushan because it controls (through shareholdings) several major Yangtze River ports in Wuhan, Chongqing, and Jiujiang. Consequently, the Port of Ningbo-Zhoushan sought to strengthen its connections with the hinterland by building dry ports. Within the network of dry ports linked to Ningbo-Zhoushan, several in the southeast have been built jointly by the ports of Xiamen and Ningbo-Zhoushan. Acting alone, the Port of Ningbo-Zhoushan has developed dry port facilities in Jinhua, Quzhou, Shaoxing, Yiwu, and Yurao. In total, the Port of Ningbo-Zhoushan has built 13 dry ports, either independently or cooperatively with other coastal ports.

By using these dry ports, the Port of Ningbo-Zhoushan has been able to cut the logistics costs of outbound cargo, thus increasing its attractiveness. As of the end of 2018, there were a total of ten regular rail services to inland dry ports, of which seven had a capacity of at least 5,000 twenty-foot equivalent units per month (table B2.10.1). An additional five rail services, though irregular, allow the Port of Ningbo-Zhoushan to serve 46 prefecture-level cities in 15 provinces across the country.

As a result of these initiatives, intermodal rail volumes have grown rapidly (see figure B2.10.1), although the share of rail in the modal split remains modest.

TABLE B2.10.1 **Selected rail service routes from the Port of Ningbo-Zhoushan, 2018**

INLAND DESTINATION(S)	TYPE OF SERVICE	RAILWAY DISTANCE (KILOMETERS)	TRIP DURATION
Shaoxing	Regular	138	5 hours
Taizhou	Regular	197	6 hours
Changxing	Regular	329	24 hours
Yiwu, Jinhua	Regular	363	20 hours
Lanxi	Regular	386	24 hours
Quzhou	Unit train	442	1–2 days
Yingtan	Regular	671	17 hours
Hefei	Regular	692	16 hours
Xuzhou	Regular	1,054	30 hours
Zhumadian	Regular	1,059	40 hours
Xiangyang	Unit train	1,359	4–5 days
Xi'an, Lanzhou	Unit train	2,393	4–5 days
Baotou	Chartered	2,471	6–7 days
Chengdu	Regular	2,692	2–3 days
Wubei, Xinjiang	Irregular	4,220	3–4 days

Source: China Waterborne Transport Research Institute (WTI).

continued

Box 2.10, *continued*

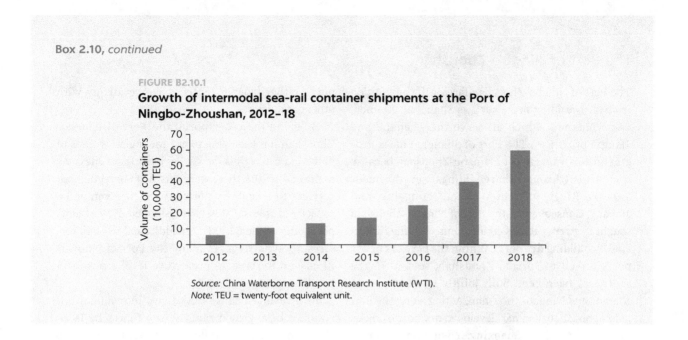

FIGURE B2.10.1

Growth of intermodal sea-rail container shipments at the Port of Ningbo-Zhoushan, 2012–18

Source: China Waterborne Transport Research Institute (WTI).
Note: TEU = twenty-foot equivalent unit.

TABLE 2.4 **Customs clearance measures enacted by the General Administration of Customs, 2006, 2014, and 2017**

YEAR	MEASURE ENACTED	EFFECT
2006	Local customs declaration and clearance at port	Simplified the customs clearance procedure and reduced administrative expense of customs clearance for enterprises
2014	Regional customs clearance integration	Improved the efficiency of customs clearance by reducing the number of customs checks needed; on average, nine hours were saved through integrated customs clearance
2017	National customs clearance integration	Simplified and standardized customs enforcement nationwide and improved customs clearance efficiency

Source: China Waterborne Transport Research Institute (WTI).

clearance integration, transfer procedures for prequalified enterprises with inbound or outbound cargo are simplified. Cargo needs to be examined only once before being transferred directly to its destination, transiting through different jurisdictions without requiring additional customs checks and using information and communication technology (ICT) platforms to track its movement. Enterprises can also choose to declare their tax and duty liabilities and make the necessary payments at inland dry ports.

In 2017, the General Administration of Customs introduced a new national customs regime, with the objective of standardizing customs enforcement and improving customs clearance nationwide (KPMG 2017). Under this new regime, customs policies will be consistently enforced across all ports, whereas previously the same goods may have been subject to different taxes at different ports, depending on the way the rules were interpreted by the regional customs authority. As a result, the efficiency of customs clearance is expected to improve because most imported goods will be released after an automatic system review, with less than 10 percent of imports requiring a manual review of customs declaration documents. Enterprises are also encouraged to make tax filings and payments at their own local dry ports, even if they are importing or exporting goods through a more distant seaport.

ENVIRONMENTAL POLICIES FOR PORTS

Ports generate a diverse set of environmental effects on air, soil, water, and natural habitats. They also produce noise, stench, and dust. This report does not aspire to provide a comprehensive discussion of all pertinent policies. Instead, this section focuses on policies to reduce air pollution generated by ports and ships, given that air pollution is widely regarded as the most important adverse environmental impact of ports (Sornn-Friese et al. 2021).

Ships are significant sources of pollution in port cities, releasing contaminants such as nitrogen oxides, sulfur oxides, and particulate matter, and greenhouse gases such as carbon dioxide and methane. Since 2006, the government of China has increased environmental protection by enacting and implementing several policies. The 11th Five-Year Plan (2006–10) called for a 10 percent reduction in total emissions of major pollutants, while the 12th Five-Year Plan (2011–15) specified reductions in sulfur dioxide and nitrous oxides of 8 percent and 10 percent, respectively, and a 17 percent decrease in carbon dioxide emissions per unit of GDP. In addition, various environmental laws were made more stringent and enforced more regularly, including the environmental protection law, the marine environmental protection law, the energy conservation law, the circular economy promotion law, and the environmental impact assessment law. Other recent action plans include the air pollution prevention and control action plan (October 2013), the water pollution prevention and control action plan (April 2015), enhanced actions on climate change (June 2015), and an updated air pollution control law (August 2015).

In addition to these general laws on environmental protection and climate change, strategies aimed specifically at regulating emissions from shipping have also been developed. The national Green Port program, which evaluates and certifies ports' overall environmental performance, was implemented in April 2015. The latest national air quality standards, which took effect in January 2016, tightened standards for particulate emissions and gave the MoT responsibility for implementing regional emission control zones. The Law on the Prevention and Control of Atmospheric Pollution added specific requirements for ships, covering fuel quality, engine standards, and the use of shore power. In addition, the MoT laid out strategies for controlling ship and port emissions in its Specialized Action Plan of Ship and Port Pollution Prevention and Control from 2015 to 2020, which defines specific goals and actions for the 2015–20 period and sets up domestic emission control zones.

Under the Green Port program, China has adopted green technologies and management measures. These include the following:

Green port standards. Standards by which to evaluate and rate green port performance are being implemented.

Use of shore power. Berthed ships are required to use shore power to reduce emissions. The Specialized Action Plan of Ship and Port Pollution Prevention and Control from 2015 to 2020 called for 90 percent of China's major ports to provide shore power for berthed ships, and 50 percent of terminals of all types (container, roll-on/roll-off, passenger, and cruise) to be capable of using shore power by 2020. A special fund was set up, and ¥ 743 million in financial support was provided to more than 200 projects. As of the end of June 2019, 3,700 systems to supply shore power had been constructed nationwide, and 5,200 terminals had supply capabilities, reaching 57 percent of the 2020 target set in the Port Shore Power Layout Plan.[7] Following initiatives to increase the availability of shore power, China also introduced stricter requirements for its use. Since July 1, 2019, vessels engaged in international voyages that have the ability to receive shore power (except tankers or vessels using "equivalent measures") have been required to use shore power if berthed for longer than three hours. As of January 1, 2021, cruise ships are required to use shore power when berthed for longer than three hours in a berth where shore power is available (photo 2.4).

Ship emission control zones to reduce emissions of air pollutants. Ship emission control zones took effect in the Yangtze River Delta in April 2016 and in the Pearl River Delta and Bohai Sea in January 2017 (map 2.5). In 2019, the zones were extended to the national coastal territorial waters. Once a ship enters a control zone, it must switch to a fuel with less than 0.5 percent sulfur content, as compared with the global maximum, which was 3.5 percent sulfur content up to January 1, 2021.[8] China has introduced more stringent measures in some areas. For example, as of January 1, 2022, a sulfur cap of 0.1 percent is being applied to seagoing vessels entering Hainan waters within the coastal emission control zones; the same applies to designated "inland control areas," including the navigable waters of the Yangtze River main lines and the Xijiang River main lines.

Switching from oil to electricity for rubber-tired container gantry cranes. Between 2015 and 2020, 2,300 rubber-tired container gantry cranes switched to electricity, resulting in a reduction in port diesel consumption of about 250,000 tons per year.

PHOTO 2.4

Wind power, Port of Wuxi

Source: © VCG. Used with the permission of VCG. Further permission required for reuse.

MAP 2.5

Ship emission control zone regions in China

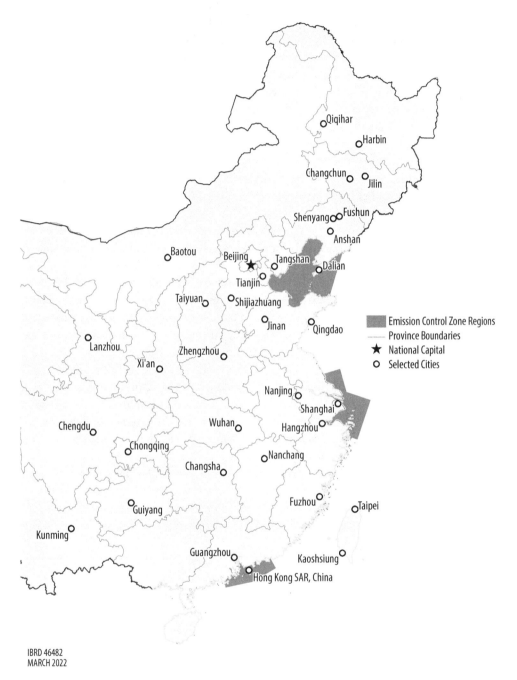

IBRD 46482
MARCH 2022

Source: World Bank, based on International Council on Clean Transportation 2016.
Note: ECZs = emission control zones.

UPGRADING SKILLS AND DIGITAL TECHNOLOGY CAPABILITIES IN PORTS

Since the 1980s, China has implemented policies to upgrade skills and technological capabilities in response to digitalization. At that time, the MoT began to explore changes to port management systems that could enhance operational efficiency. In 1987, the ministry introduced a preliminary plan for new employee contracts in large- and medium-size construction, transportation, and port enterprises. A similar system implemented in the agriculture sector in the 1970s had raised agricultural productivity throughout the country. In the port sector, the system specified the responsibilities of employees, from foremen and low-level team leaders to mid-level officials. If employees exceeded the skills specified in their contracts, they became eligible for bonuses. The incentives were introduced in a few ports before becoming more widely applied.

More changes occurred as ports began to serve both public and private shipping companies. Shekou Industrial Zone played a leading role in introducing reforms to port management systems. It did away with lifelong employment as well as egalitarian remuneration plans, instead providing incentives for fast and efficient workers. It brought about remuneration reform through the adoption of variable wages, piece rate wages, and commissions for cargo loading and unloading. The success of its market-oriented incentives, as evidenced by increased efficiency, encouraged other ports to adopt remuneration reforms.

In July 1983, Shekou Industrial Zone, founded in Shenzhen in 1979 by China Merchants Group, took the lead in breaking with uniform remuneration plans, implementing a wage system with a basic wage plus floating wages, a system more suitable for the market economy. At the outset, workers had lacked the motivation to work efficiently, with each person moving only 20–30 carloads of earth in an eight-hour workday. To provide incentives to workers, the engineering department implemented a reward system based on minimum and extra production. Each worker was now required to move a minimum of 55 carloads a day at the rate of ¥ 0.02 per cart. For each carload above the minimum, workers could earn ¥ 0.04. This motivated them to move 80 to 90 carloads per day, on average, with some moving much more.

The practice was soon halted by a superior government department. To prove that the wage system promoted efficiency, China Merchants Group invited a reporter from the Xinhua News Agency to write an internal report that was sent directly to the party general secretary. A day later, the reward system in Shekou was reinstated.

In addition, beginning in March 1982, Shekou Industrial Zone publicly recruited talent from colleges and universities, discarding the practice of senior leaders assigning workers to positions, thereby pioneering reform of the personnel system.

Modernization of port operations and management systems, with the attendant adoption of new technologies and upgrades in vessels and equipment, required ever-higher skills up, down, and across organizations. Reforms in the education system were needed to meet the growing demand for a skilled workforce. At the same time, science and technology were receiving greater priority in efforts to modernize the country.

Since 1977, China had had a merit-based system for selecting university students, based on a unified entrance exam. Although most universities are administered entirely by the Ministry of Education, some specialized maritime universities are run jointly by the Ministry of Education and the MoT. Examples are Dalian Maritime University, Shanghai Maritime University, Wuhan University of Technology, Jimei University, Chongqing Jiaotong University,

Zhejiang Ocean University, Guangdong Ocean University, Qingdao Ocean Shipping Mariners College, and Tianjin Maritime College.

Skills can also be acquired through vocational training. In 2015, both the MoT and the Ministry of Education sought to expand vocational training programs, releasing a series of regulations and advisories, including the Opinions of the Ministry of Transport and the Ministry of Education on Developing Vocational Education in the Modern Transportation Sector (Ministry of Transport and Ministry of Education 2016). Part-time educational courses were made available to further enhance and upgrade workers' skill sets. In addition to education and skills training, the MoT funds scientific research. At present, 26 industrial laboratories conduct research in water transport. In addition, maritime and logistics courses are supported by port cities, for example, at the University of Ningbo.

Port companies are labor intensive, requiring significant manpower and skilled workers. Port employees can be roughly classified into three types: production operators, technicians and engineers, and administrators. According to a 2018 analysis by the China Waterborne Transport Research Institute (WTI) on regular employees of 12 listed port companies in coastal areas, operational and technical workers account for, on average, about 72 percent of the total (figure 2.16). In this group, production operators represent a larger share than technical engineers (about 57 percent and 15 percent, respectively). The analysis also showed that, on average, about 31 percent of port employees hold at least a bachelor's degree.

FIGURE 2.16

Proportion of operational and technical workers, and of staff with bachelor's degree and higher at specific ports, 2018

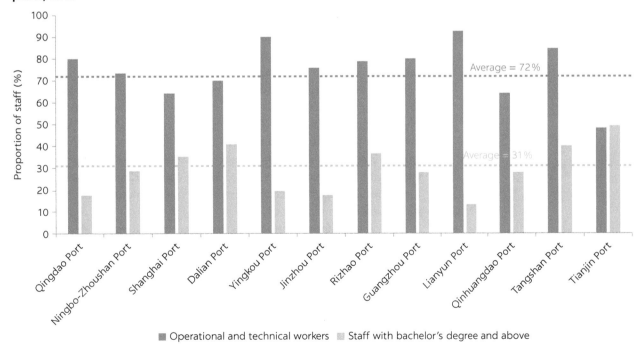

Sources: Analysis by China Waterborne Transport Research Institute (WTI), based on port group annual reports for 2019, as follows: Dalian Port Group 2020; Guangzhou Port Group 2020; Lianyun Port Group 2020; Ningbo-Zhoushan Port Group 2020; Qingdao Port Group 2020; Qinhuangdao Port Group 2020; Rizhao Port Group 2020; Shanghai International Port Group 2020; Tianjin Port Group 2020; Yingkou Port Group 2020.

Production operators can be recruited from colleges and universities, vocational and technical schools, or labor service companies. They do not usually need a degree; if they possess the necessary professional skills, they can be trained on the job. In contrast, most technicians and engineers generally hold a university degree because they perform skilled jobs that require specific technical or professional training.

Port companies in China regard training as an important way to increase operational efficiency, promote safety, improve quality, and cultivate talent. Many companies have established internal training centers equipped with modern multimedia training facilities. They offer off- and online training courses and ensure the continuity of their training programs.

The Shanghai Port Group and others also offer employee ownership plans to encourage employee loyalty and dedication. The group also provides equity incentives to professional managers to improve their motivation.

Digitalization initiatives

ICT is now an important part of all industries, including those connected to the port sector. Global trade competition has driven ports and logistics firms to invest in new technologies such as the Internet of Things, big data, cloud computing, and artificial intelligence (Karimpour and Karimpour 2018). The COVID-19 pandemic has further heightened interest in automation and digitalization. Proper use of these technologies can solve complex problems in multiple port domains and activities, optimizing processes and increasing ports' resiliency as key enablers of global trade. Technology can also help the workforce make better decisions. Port authorities and governments can help ensure the coordinated development and integration of ICT systems throughout the port and logistics sector.

In China, ICT platforms began to be applied in ports in the 1980s, when the move toward an export-oriented economy led to a huge increase in the volume of imports and exports and of container shipments. To deal with growing demand, technologies were implemented to increase the efficiency of container transport. Several major ports, such as Guangzhou, Shanghai, and Tianjin, adopted computer applications and operating systems developed in other countries (for example, Japan, the Republic of Korea, and the United Kingdom) and used them to plan and implement container operations, including loading, unloading, storage, booking, and dispatch. At the same time, these ports installed information management systems to improve daily port operations. Local ICT companies also began to develop their own patented terminal operating systems, which were used in smaller ports.

These initial efforts to introduce ICT were carried out independently by individual ports, resulting in isolated systems. Data could not be shared across platforms owing to limited technology and weak communications infrastructure. The systems were used chiefly to digitize paperwork and replace manual data processing, with few other value-added services.

In 1984, the MoT set up a computer applications group to coordinate the construction of ICT systems for road and waterborne transport. In 1987, in response to the need to modernize the transport management system, it issued Overall Planning for Transport Economical Information Systems, which offered guidance on the unified planning and construction of transport ICT systems, including those for ports (Zheng 1994). The challenge was the proliferation of unlinked individual systems that thwarted coordination of the entire system.

In the mid-1990s, rapid development of the national economy greatly increased demand for specialized terminals and transport facilities, which in turn led to increased demand for port informatics. ICT systems were developed that improved production and operational efficiency, and the use of ICT was extended from container terminals to bulk and oil terminals. Port information technology had five features during this period. The first was an emphasis on introducing electronic data interchange to automate, digitize, process, and transmit documents related to all aspects of container transport. Its development was promoted by the MoT, which carried out the International Container Transport Electronic Data Interchange (EDI) and Operation System and Demonstration Project in 1995 through centers at Ningbo, Qingdao, Shanghai, and Tianjin (Ministry of Transport 1995). Second, management information systems were developed in various specialized terminals. Individual ports built or modified these systems based on their individual needs, developing applications for dry bulk and reefer terminals, as well as oil and ore terminals. Software for advanced container terminal operations was also introduced to provide real-time control of on-site operations. Third, strong business management systems were applied in the areas of finance, human resources, procurement, and equipment management. Fourth, to achieve real-time control of field operations and uninterrupted communication of information, ports began to establish computer-server clusters with enough bandwidth to support advanced ICT systems. Finally, ports began to acquire and cultivate highly skilled professionals to continue the development and management of these ICT systems.

Until 2005, individual ports had been introducing ICT innovations independently, with new technologies adopted as needed, but with little integration. Regulations and advisories from the MoT—such as a framework for cataloging highway and waterway information resources in January 2007 (Ministry of Transport 2006) and the Eleventh Five-Year Development Plan for Highway and Waterway Traffic Informatization in May 2007 (Ministry of Transport 2007a)—decried the duplication of transport information systems and the lack of system compatibility, interconnectivity, and information sharing.

The 11th Five-Year Plan (2006–10) called for an enhancement of ports' ability to collect dynamic traffic information, such as real-time ship movements at ports and in waterways and the remote monitoring of operations and special vessels (such as those carrying dangerous goods). The MoT also called for comprehensive information sharing between ports, customs, and hinterland transport modes, as well as between government, logistics service providers, and the industrial and commercial enterprises generating the cargo.

In response, China's ports began to focus on creating unified management and operations centers, as well as logistics and e-commerce service platforms that featured information sharing and all-in-one services. Ports established integrated operating models that unified heretofore disparate units. Major ports also began to extend the coverage of ICT systems from terminal operations to logistics. New logistics and e-commerce platforms integrated transaction, logistics, and online payment functions. ICT systems for shipping agencies, freight forwarding companies, and container management services were also developed. By integrating these systems into a single platform, ports could coordinate information and financial flows throughout the entire supply chain, improving efficiency and transparency while lowering costs. Recent examples from two ports appear in box 2.11.

As with the rest of the world, China's maritime trade and economic growth slowed following the 2008 global financial crisis. The early focus on port construction had led to overcapacity in ports, but also to intense competition between them. The shift in the balance of power toward shipping companies and cargo owners pushed ports to introduce client-oriented services. At the same time, increases in ship size (especially container ships) were straining ports' collection and distribution systems.

These challenges further motivated China's port sector to embrace new technologies. After 2011, ports began to apply the Internet of Things, cloud computing, and big data, among others, to develop high-end services and further increase their competitiveness. The Twelfth Five-Year Development Plan for Highway and Waterway Traffic Informatization (2011–15) called for the continuous integration of information resources, but also highlighted the expansion of ICT systems into other parts of the logistics network (such as the hinterland transport systems), as well as the use of ICT for monitoring safety and security in transport networks and ports (Ministry of Transport 2011).

To date, innovations include terminal automation, collaborative logistics chains, and big data usage. By accumulating system operations data, port enterprises are capable of big-data-driven analysis, thereby proactively providing the

---

BOX 2.11

Two examples of digitalization initiatives from the ports of Xiamen and Shanghai

Xiamen: Digitalization of documentation

The Port of Xiamen introduced a digital equipment identity register system in 2016, after two years of research and development. A digital equipment identity register minimizes, if not eliminates, repeated entry. It has eliminated huge numbers of staff for document preparation and delivery and who work at the gate, thus significantly reducing the cost of labor. In total, the digital transformation has benefited 13 shipping companies, 48 yards outside the port, 514 transportation companies (with 9,981 vehicles and 9,182 drivers registered), 6 terminal companies, and 1 inland port. As the equipment identity register turns digital, the efficiency of information exchange has been enhanced significantly between the terminals and stations, logistics parks, inland ports, and port authorities. Based on the system, the dispatch of on-site trailers can be more efficient, thus cutting management costs for vehicles, relieving road congestion within the port, and contributing remarkably to energy savings

and emissions reduction. At the terminal gate, document handover is now based on an automatic identification system and in digital form instead of on paper, raising traffic efficiency by 67 percent. Currently, most of China's major coastal ports have transformed to paperless on-site operations mode.

Shanghai: Collaboration between river and ocean transport, and between port and city

Shanghai is the world's largest container port. Because much of its throughput is moved inland through the waterway system along the Yangtze River, the Port of Shanghai has built an operations platform for river-sea transport that includes systems for loading, unloading, and customs processing (photo B2.11.1). The platform enables all transport partners to visualize the entire logistics process.

A collaborative platform for container collection and distribution has also been developed. Users can

continued

Box 2.11, *continued*

Inland container barges operating at the automated container terminal at Yangshan, Port of Shanghai

Source: © VCG. Used with the permission of VCG. Further permission required for reuse.

make online reservations to move their containers into the yards. Each container has an electronic tag, allowing it to be identified automatically. Equipment handover documents and container pickup receipts are also transmitted digitally, resulting in faster circulation of documents, reduced waiting times at the port gates, and less road congestion around the terminal.

services that clients require. The sharing and exchange of information through the logistics network also improves collaboration and can improve the efficiency of the supply chain. ICT innovations are part of the sustainable development of ports, allowing for easier monitoring of equipment, facilities, personnel, and operations, and dynamically identifying possible risks and security issues (box 2.12). Even before the COVID-19 pandemic, the shift toward automation and digitalization was inevitable.

Table 2.5 describes the functions of ICT systems at some of the major ports in China.

Development of an integrated single window

One way to reduce the administrative burden of cross-border trade is through the single window, defined as "a facility that allows parties involved in trade and

Current goals of information and communication technology development in China's ports

China's ports are pursuing the following goals for information and communication technology development.

Paperless port operations. All key port businesses—including cargo handling and customs services—will use an electronic format for documents to facilitate transfers of information through the logistics chain, eliminate manual handling, and reduce fraud.

Sharing of documents across the logistics chain. Efficient and coordinated operations, and resource integration within the port logistics network, are two priorities. Through digital supply chain systems, cargo owners, freight forwarders, train operators, road carriers, terminal yards, and other enterprises can use a single platform to share information and complete necessary tasks, including business acceptance, whole-journey tracking, account verification, and payment settlements. China aims to have more than 90 percent of relevant business documents standardized and shared between the different companies.

Automation. China's ports have built intelligent systems for gate control, tallying, equipment dispatching, and ship scheduling. Advanced digital technology has been applied to port production systems, developing intelligent port operations, and refining safety management. Examples include fully automated container terminals in the Qingdao, Shanghai, and Xiamen ports, and fully automated coal terminals in Huangqi and Qinhuangdao. China aims to have more than 90 percent of key port businesses controlled remotely or managed by automation.

24/7 safety supervision. A tracking system for dangerous cargo will be constructed with 100 percent visual surveillance throughout the logistics chain.

Seamless multimodal transport. Different transport modes will be connected seamlessly by multimodal transport operators. Demonstration projects financed by the Ministry of Transport include one on information sharing and Internet of Things applications for rail-water container transport at six major ports (2012), and another on smart systems for safety management (2017).

Online customer information and service. China's ports aim to achieve 100 percent online operations for customer services, including the handling of customer inquiries, reservations, document acceptance, and electronic payments. Logistics information such as storage yard location, gate records, container truck movements, port release documents, cargo loading and unloading records, and ship information will all be stored and accessible online. Users will be provided with mobile and visual logistics information and services.

Collaboration between ports. China aims to set up a platform for data exchange between ports, shared with the regulatory authorities. The data will include more than 90 percent of port operations, such as customs declarations and inspections.

Energy conservation and green operations. Smart infrastructure will be used to improve energy efficiency and maximize the use of renewable energy.

transport to lodge standardized information and documents with a single-entry point to fulfil all import, export, and transit-related regulatory requirements" (United Nations Economic Commission for Europe 2005, 3). In other words, a single-window system aims to expedite and simplify information flows between trade and government, bringing economic integration and meaningful gains to all parties involved in cross-border trade. Whenever information is electronic, it is recommended that data elements should need to be submitted only once. Single-window platforms have been initiated in several countries across the globe, each one subject to different political, economic, or legal circumstances. The approach applies to data exchange among government agencies and between private firms and government agencies.

China has developed an integrated, national single-window system in the course of various customs reforms. In March 1988, a milestone project was

TABLE 2.5 **Information and communication technology systems in major ports of China**

PORT	SYSTEM	FEATURES
Dalian	Dalian Port and Waterway Community System	Fast and accurate information about shipping services, berth assignments, import manifests, and other documents, as well as forwarding, electronic payment, and settlement services for logistics customers such as shipping companies or agents, transport fleets, and cargo agents
Tianjin	Port Logistics Integrated Service Platform	One-stop online processing of booking space, multimodal transport, distribution, cargo tracking, payment, and settlement, and a unified window for the external services of various port businesses
Qingdao	Port Logistics Electronic Commerce Service System	One-stop logistics solution and online business operation platform, setting service standards across the logistics network
Shanghai	River-Sea Combined Transportation Integrated Service Platform	Unified online cargo acceptance, job progress inquiry, information inquiry, evaluation, complaint management, and other functions
Ningbo-Zhoushan	Port Logistics Information Platform	Integration of various business platforms, including inland port resources, container transportation network, and value-added logistics services inside and outside the port
Xiamen	Intelligent Collection and Distribution Coordination Platform	Integration and information sharing for all logistics entities in the port related to customer bookings, trailer commissions, container pickups, special-area entry declarations, inspection reservations, entry to the port, and other logistics services
Guangzhou	Port Logistics Online Business Hall	Online business processing, payment settlements, and other customer services, with paperless processing in a one-stop system
Shenzhen	Port Unified Customer Service Platform	Information sharing and operational coordination among enterprises to improve the efficiency of port operations and reduce operating costs

Source: China Waterborne Transport Research Institute (WTI).

launched to develop the National Customs Clearance Management System (initially called H883), which aimed to automate many of the trade processing procedures of the national customs authority, the General Administration of Customs. The system gradually replaced many manual operations with computerized trade processing for procedures such as vehicle monitoring, trade-related certificate verification, trade management, license management, and tariff exemption.

In 1998, the General Administration of Customs began exploring an interagency verification system for joint monitoring of trade-related supply chains. This system would form the core application of a new system called E-port, which served as the basis for the creation of a nationwide integrated single-window environment. A first step involved the development of a high-level design layout, based on the E-port platforms. This step was followed by the implementation of functions related to port regulation, integrating systems from businesses and cross-border regulatory agencies at the central level (Wu 2011). The third stage expanded on functions related to port services at a business-to-business level. The last stage, still in progress, involves actively promoting single-window cooperation at the transboundary level, connecting with other nations' trade facilitation tools.

China's national single window, which meets relevant standards established by the World Consumer Protection Organization and the United Nations Centre for Trade Facilitation and Electronic Business, connects with the business systems of 25 cross-border regulatory agencies at the central level and promotes information sharing among them. Applicants can gain access to the single-window system at a single entry point and submit standardized documents and electronic information that meet the requirements of cross-border regulatory agencies. Information on the status or outcome of applications can be transmitted to applicants through the system.

The integration of systems has increased clearance efficiency, reduced data redundancies, and streamlined data transmission requirements because data can now be recorded and shared electronically with all relevant parties. Whereas previously each step in the customs clearance process was performed in isolation, the single window allows for a one-time declaration and more efficient processing. Following the simplification and merging of data, the number of documents required for processing customs declarations has dropped from 89 to 52. Customs clearance time has dropped by more than 40 percent, significantly cutting businesses' costs.

NOTES

1. A circular economy is based on the principles of designing out waste and pollution, keeping products and materials in use, and regenerating natural systems.
2. Administrative functions included pilotage and maritime safety, whereas enterprise functions were more concerned with port operations and services.
3. In this period, measures were also taken to ensure that China's port sector met international standards. China issued its first maritime traffic safety law in 1983, setting up a maritime safety supervision department in each port. These departments reported directly to the MoT and were responsible for maritime traffic management, maritime search and rescue, construction and maintenance of navigation buoys, maritime wireless communications, and other international requirements established by the International Maritime Organization. The establishment of these safety departments was one of the first steps taken to separate ports' administrative functions from their business operations, leading to the founding of the Maritime Safety Administration in 1996.
4. If a port incurred a deficit, the loan would be considered a subsidy.
5. Large diesel-powered vehicles are responsible for 60 percent of the nitrogen oxides and 85 percent of the particulate pollution released on China's roads, despite making up only 8 percent of all vehicles.
6. The terms "inland port" and "dry port" are often used interchangeably in the literature. While every effort has been made to standardize the terminology in this report, some port names may use inland port rather than dry port.
7. Technical difficulties arise because the electrical systems on most international vessels operate at 60 hertz (Hz), whereas the frequency in Chinese ports is 50 Hz, so frequency converters must be installed.
8. In line with most ports around the globe, China has prohibited the discharge of wash water from open-loop scrubbers in most ports and inland rivers.

REFERENCES

Abdoulkarim, Hamadou Tahirou, Seydou Harouna Fatouma, and Elijah Musango Munyao. 2019. "Dry Ports in China and West Africa: A Comparative Study." *American Journal of Industrial and Business Management* 9 (3): 448–67.

Aritua, Bernard, Lu Cheng, Richard van Liere, and Harrie de Leijer. 2020. *Blue Routes for a New Era.* Washington, DC: World Bank.

Beijing Customs and Tianjin Customs. 1994. "Implementation Plan on Supervision of Direct Port-to-Port Links along Beijing-Tianjin-Tanggu Expressway." Policy Note, Beijing Customs and Tianjin Customs.

Bury, Ben, and Joshua Leung. 2020. "Ports & Terminals in China." Lexology. March 14, 2020. https://www.lexology.com/gtdt/tool/workareas/report/ports-and-terminals/chapter/china.

Cao, Pu. 2001. "Gu Mu and the Opening Up of China to the Outside World in 1978–1988." *Hundred Year Tide* 11. 谷牧与 1978-1988 年的中国对外开放 (in Chinese).

China Internet Information Center. n.d. "A Brief Introduction of National Economic and Technological Development Zones in China." http://www.china.org.cn/english /SPORT-c/76751.htm.

CMSK (China Merchants Shekou Industrial Zone Holdings). n.d. "Corporate Overview." https://www.cmsk1979.com/en/about.aspx.

Crane, Bret, Chad Albrecht, Kristopher McKay Duffin, and Conan Albrecht. 2018. "China's Special Economic Zones: An Analysis of Policy to Reduce Regional Disparities." *Regional Studies, Regional Science* 5 (1): 98–107.

Cullinane, Kevin, and Teng-Fei Wang. 2006. "Port Governance in China." *Research in Transportation Economics* 17: 331–56.

Dalian Port Group. 2020. "Dalian Port Group Annual Report of 2019." http://data.eastmoney .com/notices/detail/02880/AN202003261377005446,JUU1JUE0JUE3JUU 4JUJGJTlFJUU2JUI4JUFG.html.

Fang, Chuanglin. 2015. "Important Progress and Future Direction of Studies on China's Urban Agglomerations." *Journal of Geographic Sciences* 25 (8): 1003–24.

Grogan, Bryan. 2019. "This Day in History: The Founding of Shekou Industrial Zone." *That's*, January 31. https://www.thatsmags.com/shanghai/post/26789/this-day-in-history -the-founding-of-shekou-industrial-zone.

Guan, Changqian, and Shmuel Yahalom. 2011. "China's Port Reform and Development: Policy Analysis." *Transportation Research Record* 2222 (1): 1–9.

Guangzhou Port Group. 2020. "Guangzhou Port Group Annual Report of 2019." http://quotes .money.163.com/f10/ggmx_601228_5980088.html.

Hanson, Arthur. 2019. "Ecological Civilization in the People's Republic of China: Values, Action, and Future Needs." ADB East Asia Working Paper Series 21, Asian Development Bank, Manila.

Herlevi, April A. 2016. "What's So Special about Special Economic Zones? China's National and Provincial-Level Development Zones." Department of Politics, University of Virginia, Charlottesville.

Hofman, Bert. 2018. "Reflections on Forty Years of China's Reforms—Speech at the Fudan University's Fanhai School of International Finance." In *China's 40 Years of Reform and Development: 1978–2018*, edited by Ross Garnaut, Ligang Song, and Cai Fang, 53–66. Acton, Australia: Australian National University Press.

International Council on Clean Transportation. 2016. "Action Plan for Establishing Ship Emission Control Zones in China." https://theicct.org/publications/action-plan -establishing-ship-emission-control-zones-china.

Jinzhou Port Group. 2020. "Jinzhou Port Group Annual Report of 2019." http://data.eastmoney .com/notices/detail/600190/AN201908261345117555.html.

Karimpour, Reza, and Maryam Karimpour. 2018. "Digitalisation and ICT innovations—A Focus on Port Logistics." Docks the Future. May 21, 2018. https://www.docksthefuture.eu /digitalisation-and-ict-innovations-a-focus-on-port-logistics/.

KPMG. 2017. "China Customs Authority Implements National Customs Clearance Integration Regime Reform." China Tax Alert. August 10, 2017. https://home.kpmg/cn/en/home /insights/2017/08/china-tax-alert-24.html.

Lawrence, Martha, Richard Bullock, and Ziming Liu. 2019. *China's High-Speed Rail Development*. Washington, DC: World Bank.

Lemoine, Françoise, Grégoire Mayo, Sandra Poncet, and Deniz Ünal. 2014. "The Geographic Pattern of China's Growth and Convergence within Industry." Working Paper, Centre d'Etudes Prospectives et d'Informations Internationales, Paris.

Lianyun Port Group. 2020. "Lianyun Port 2019 Annual Report." https://data.eastmoney.com /notices/detail/601008/AN202003261377010152.html.

Livermore, Adam. 2007. "Investors Guide to the Dalian Development Zone." China Briefing. October 1, 2007. https://www.china-briefing.com/news/investors-guide-to-the-dalian -development-zone/.

Ministry of Communications. 1985. "Implementation Rules of the Measures for the Collection of Port Construction Fees" (in Chinese). Beijing. http://www.chinalawedu.com/falvfagui /fg22016/18178.shtml.

Ministry of Railways. 2003. "Mid- and Long-Term Railway Network Plan." Beijing. http://www .gov.cn/ztzl/2005-09/16/content_64413.htm.

Ministry of Transport. 1992. "Opinions on Deepening Reform, Expanding Opening Up and Accelerating Transportation Development." Beijing. http://www.law020.com/fagui/public _sauuwcx.html.

Ministry of Transport. 1995. "The International Container Transport EDI and Operation System and Demonstration Project." Policy Note, Ministry of Transport, Beijing.

Ministry of Transport. 2001. "Notice on the Issuance of Highway and Waterway Traffic Fifteen Development Plan," 关于印发公路水路交通十五发展计划的通知 (in Chinese). Beijing. https://www.chinacourt.org/law/detail/2001/07/id/81136.shtml.

Ministry of Transport. 2003. "Mandate on Speeding Up the Separation of Government and Port Enterprises and Strengthening Port Administration," 关于加快港口政企分开步伐和加强港口行政管理的通知 (in Chinese). Beijing.

Ministry of Transport. 2006. "Guiding Opinions on Strengthening the Development and Utilization of Transportation Information Resources," 关于印发公路水路信息资源目录体系总体框架的通知 (in Chinese). Beijing. http://xxgk.mot.gov.cn/jigou/kjs/201304 /t20130412_2974911.html.

Ministry of Transport. 2007a. "Eleventh Five-Year Development Plan for Highway and Waterway Traffic Informatization," 公路水路交通信息化"十一五"发展规划 (in Chinese). Beijing. http://xxgk.mot.gov.cn/jigou/zhghs/201811/t20181116_3129290.html.

Ministry of Transport. 2007b. "Layout Plan of National Inland Waterways and Ports," 全国内河港口和航道规划 (in Chinese). Beijing. http://www.gov.cn/gzdt/2007-07/20/content_691664 .htm.

Ministry of Transport. 2011. "Twelfth Five-Year Development Plan for Highway and Waterway Traffic Informatization," 公路水路交通信息化"十二五"发展规划 (in Chinese). Beijing. http:// www.gov.cn/gongbao/content/2011/content_1992578.htm.

Ministry of Transport. 2017. "Thirteenth Five-Year Development Plan for Highway and Waterway Traffic Informatization," 公路水路交通信息化"十三五"发展规划 (in Chinese). Beijing. http://www.gov.cn/zhengce/content/2017-02/28/content_5171345.htm.

Ministry of Transport. 2018. *China Transport Statistical Yearbook 2018*. Beijing: China Communications Press.

Ministry of Transport. 2019. *40 Years of China's Opening-Up and Reform*. Beijing: Ministry of Transport.

Ministry of Transport. 2022. "Fourteenth Five-Year Development Plan for Modern Integrated Transport System," 十四五"现代综合交通运输体系发展规划 (in Chinese). Beijing. https:// xxgk.mot.gov.cn/2020/jigou/zhghs/202201/t20220119_3637245.html.

Ministry of Transport and Ministry of Education. 2016. "Opinions on Accelerating the Development of Modern Transportation Vocational Education," 加快发展现代交通运输职业教育的若干意见 (in Chinese). Beijing. https://xxgk.mot.gov.cn/2020/jigou/rsjys/202006 /t20200623_3311457.html.

Ministry of Transport and National Development and Reform Commission. 2015. "Port Charges and Charges Measures." Beijing. http://www.waizi.org.cn/law/8653.html.

Ministry of Transport and National Development and Reform Commission. 2019. "Notice on the Revision and Issuance of the Measures for Port Charges." Beijing. http://www.gov.cn /gongbao/content/2019/content_5411613.htm.

National Bureau of Statistics of China. 2004–2019. *China Statistical Yearbook*. China Statistics Press.

National Development and Reform Commission. 2017. "Notice on Deepening Market-Oriented Reform of Railway Freight Prices and Other Related Issues," 关于深化铁路货运价格市场化改革等有关问题的通知 (in Chinese). Beijing. http://www.gov.cn/xinwen/2017-12/26 /content_5250421.htm.

Ningbo-Zhoushan Port Group. 2020. "Ningbo Zhoushan Port Co. 2019 Annual Report." http://data.eastmoney.com/notices/detail/601018/AN202004101377881975,JUU1JUFFJTgxJUU2JUIzJUEyJUU2JUI4JUI4JUFG.html.

Notteboom, Theo, and Zhongzhen Yang. 2017. "Port Governance in China since 2004: Institutional Layering and the Growing Impact of Broader Policies." *Research in Transportation Business and Management* 22: 184–200.

Qingdao Port Group. 2020. "Qingdao Port International Co. Annual Report 2019." http://data.eastmoney.com/notices/detail/06198/AN202003261377004111,JWU5JTlkJTkyJWU1JWIyJTliJWU2JWI4JWI4JWFm.html.

Qinhuangdao Port Group. 2020. "Qinhuangdao Port 2019 Annual Report." https://q.stock.sohu.com/newpdf/202038854794.pdf.

Qiu, Min. 2008. "Coastal Port Reform in China." *Maritime Policy and Management* 35 (2): 175–91.

Rizhao Port Group. 2020. "Rizhao Port Group Annual Report of 2019." http://quotes.money.163.com/f10/ggmx_600017_5957730.html.

Roehrig, Michael F. 1994. *Foreign Joint Ventures in Contemporary China*. New York: St. Martin's Press.

Shanghai International Port Group. 2020. "Shanghai Port Group Annual Report 2019." http://quotes.money.163.com/f10/ggmx_600018_6014075.html.

Song, Xiaowu, Shiguo Wu, and Xin Xu. 2019. *The Great Change in the Regional Economy of China under the New Normal*. Singapore: Springer Nature.

Sornn-Friese, Henrik, René Tauda Poulsen, Agnieszka Urszula Nowinska, and Peter de Langen. 2021. "What Drives Ports around the World to Adopt Air Emissions Abatement Measures?" *Transportation Research Part D: Transport and Environment* 90.

SPC, SETC, and MoFTEC (State Planning Commission, State Economic and Trade Commission, and Ministry of Foreign Trade and Economic Cooperation). 1995. "Catalogue for the Guidance of Foreign Investment Industries" (in Chinese). Ministry of Commerce of the PRC, Beijing. http://www.mofcom.gov.cn/aarticle/b/f/200207/20020700031063.html.

SPC, SETC, and MoFTEC (State Planning Commission, State Economic and Trade Commission, and Ministry of Foreign Trade and Economic Cooperation). 2002. "Catalogue for the Guidance of Foreign Investment Industries" (in Chinese). Ministry of Commerce of the PRC, Beijing. http://wzs.mofcom.gov.cn/article/n/200208/20020800035372.shtml.

State Administration of Taxation. 1989. "Regulations of the State Administration of Taxation on the Levy and Exemption of Land Use Taxes for Port Land Used in the Transportation Sector" (in Chinese). Beijing. http://www.chinacfo.net/csfg/mj.asp?id=A2007121816216577367.

State Council. 1985a. "Interim Regulations of the State Council of the People's Republic of China on Preferential Treatment to Sino-Foreign Joint Ventures on Harbor and Wharf Construction" (in Chinese). Beijing. http://www.people.com.cn/zixun/flfgk/item/dwjjf/falv/2/2-1-08.html.

State Council. 1985b. "Measures for the Collection of Port Construction Fees" (in Chinese). Beijing. https://sz.msa.gov.cn/flfg/85453.jhtml.

State Council. 1992. "Circular of the State Council Regarding Further Reform of the Administration of International Ocean Shipping Industry," 国务院关于进一步改革国际海洋运输管理工作的通知 (in Chinese). Beijing. http://www.gov.cn/zhengce/content/2010-12/19/content_3663.htm.

State Council. 2001. "Opinions on Deepening the Reform of the Port Management System under the Direct and Dual Leadership of the Central Government" (in Chinese). Beijing. http://www.gov.cn/gongbao/content/2002/content_61548.htm.

State Council. 2004a. "Land Administration Law of the People's Republic of China (2004 Revision)." Beijing. http://www.asianlii.org/cn/legis/cen/laws/lalotproc2004r572/.

State Council. 2004b. "Port Law of the People's Republic of China." Beijing. http://www.moj.gov.cn/pub/sfbgw/flfggz/flfggzfl/202101/t20210122_150979.html.

State Council. 2014. "Opinions of Promoting the Healthy Development of the Maritime Industry," 国务院关于促进海运业健康发展的若干意见 (in Chinese). Beijing. http://www.gov.cn/zhengce/content/2014-09/03/content_9062.htm.

State Council, Ministry of Finance, Ministry of Transport, and Price Bureau. 1993. "Notice on Expanding the Collection Range of Port Construction Fees, Raising Fee Rates, and Levying Surcharges Waterborne Passengers and Freight," 关于扩大港口建设费征收范围、提高征收标准及开征水运客货运附加费的通知 (in Chinese). Beijing. http://law.esnai.com/mview/17321.

Tangshan Port Group. 2020."Tangshan Port Group Annual Report of 2019." https://www.shclearing.com.cn/xxpl/cwbg/nb/202004/t20200423_671309.html.

Tianjin Port Group. 2020. "Tianjin Port Group Annual Report of 2019." http://quotes.money.163.com/f10/ggmx_600717_5962280.html.

United Nations Economic Commission for Europe. 2005. "Recommendation and Guidelines on Establishing a Single Window to Enhance the Efficient Exchange of Information between Trade and Government." Recommendation No. 33. Centre for Trade Facilitation and Electronic Business, International Trade Procedures Working Group, United Nations, New York, Geneva.

Wang, James Jixian. 2018. *Port-City Interplays in China*. New York: Routledge.

Wang, James Jixian. 2020. "Port-City Development in China." In *Handbook on Transport and Urban Transformation in China*, edited by Chia-Lin Chen, Haixiao Pan, Qing Shen, and James J. Wang, 19–35. Cheltenham, UK: Edward Elgar.

Wang, Jin. 2013. "The Economic Impact of Special Economic Zones: Evidence from Chinese Municipalities." *Journal of Development Economics* 101: 133–47.

Wang, Lei, Zhixiang Zhou, Yang Yang, and Jie Wu. 2020. "Green Efficiency Evaluation and Improvement of Chinese Ports: A Cross-Efficiency Model." *Transportation Research Part D: Transport and Environment* 88.

Wei, Xie. 2000. "Acquisition of Technological Capability through Special Economic Zones (SEZs): The Case of Shenzhen SEZ." *Industry and Innovation* 7 (2): 199–221.

World Bank. 1982. "China—Three Ports Project." World Bank, Washington, DC. http://documents.worldbank.org/curated/en/460041468024562574/China-Three-Ports-Project.

World Bank. 2009. *World Development Report 2009: Reshaping Economic Geography*. Washington, DC: World Bank.

World Bank. 2020. *From Recovery to Rebalancing: China's Economy in 2021. China Economic Update*. Washington, DC: World Bank.

World Bank and Development Research Center of the State Council of the People's Republic of China. 2014. *Urban China: Toward Efficient, Inclusive, and Sustainable Urbanization*. Washington, DC: World Bank.

Wu, Jiang. 2011. "China Customs Information Processing System and E-Port." Shanghai Customs College.

Wu, Min, Huang Jiuli, and Liu Chong. 2021. "Special Economic Zones and Innovation: Evidence from Data." *China Economic Quarterly International* 1 (4): 319–30.

Xing, Wei, Qing Liu, and Guangjun Chen. 2018. "Pricing Strategies for Port Competition and Cooperation." *Maritime Policy and Management* 45 (2): 260–77.

Xu, Meng, and Anthony T. H. Chin. 2012. "Port Governance in China: Devolution and Effects Analysis." *Procedia—Social and Behavioral Sciences* 43: 14–23.

Yeung, Yue-man, Joanna Lee, and Gordon Kee. 2013. "China's Special Economic Zones at 30." *Eurasian Geography and Economics* 50 (2): 222–40.

Yingkou Port Group. 2020. "Yingkou Port Group Annual Report of 2019." http://quotes.money.163.com/f10/ggmx_600317_5968681.html.

Zeng, Douglas Zhihua. 2011. "How Do Special Economic Zones and Industrial Clusters Drive China's Rapid Development?" Policy Research Working Paper, World Bank, Washington, DC.

Zeng, Douglas Zhihua. 2012. "China's Special Economic Zones and Industrial Clusters: Success and Challenges." Working Paper, Lincoln Institute of Land Policy, Cambridge, MA.

Zeng, Douglas Zhihua. 2015. "Global Experiences with Special Economic Zones: Focus on China and Africa." Policy Research Working Paper, World Bank, Washington, DC.

Zheng, Guangdi. 1994. "In Progress of Transport Economical Information System." Electrical Industry Outlook and Decision Making, Beijing. doi:CNKI:SUN:DZJC.0.1994-Z1-003.

3 Lessons from China's Port Sector Development

INTRODUCTION

This chapter draws important lessons from the development of China's ports. Each lesson is accompanied by reflections on its relevance for developing countries. This report captures eight lessons in four areas:

- Macroeconomic and regional development (lessons 1 and 2, in boxes 3.1 and 3.2)
- Port-hinterland connectivity and port cities (lessons 3 and 4, in boxes 3.3 and 3.4)
- Human resources and innovation (lesson 5, in box 3.5)
- Port governance and finance (lessons 6–8, in boxes 3.6–3.8).

MACROECONOMIC AND REGIONAL DEVELOPMENT: A HOLISTIC APPROACH

Ports are a key part of business ecosystems, involving logistics, administration, processing, and even leisure activities. In China's approach, the development of ports to support export-led economic growth occurred in tandem with the formation of special economic zones (SEZs). The foreign direct investment attracted by the SEZs boosted demand for cargo handling and resulted in a high rate of utilization of newly developed terminals. Predictable and strong demand growth facilitated the transition to a more commercial approach to port development.

China's holistic approach aligned port development with policies to accelerate the economic development of interior regions as the coastal economy evolved toward services and advanced technologies. This approach enabled economic activity to spread to less-developed regions in China's hinterland. Complementary policies were adopted to support this transition, including investments in hinterland infrastructure, development of dry ports as centers for manufacturing and logistics, encouragement of ports' investment in inland

BOX 3.1

Lesson 1: Port development should not stop at the port gate

Taking a holistic approach to port development involves aligning logistics, trade, and transport policies with broader economic development strategies. In China, port development was well integrated with broader economic development planning. Port planning supported broader strategies in various ways, including integrating port development with special economic zones, inland logistics, customs administration, hinterland transport networks, and trade facilitation. Port development was conceived of as an element of the larger economy. In most emerging economies the relationship between the port and economic development goals is not as clear. However, in China the frontiers of traditional port planning were expanded to consider national economic and social objectives, opportunities for developing the hinterland, the interests of the various supply chains that pass through the port, and the community within which each port is embedded. China's experience shows the importance of this holistic approach.

Because most ports are now part of national and global supply chains, successful planning must extend far beyond the port gate and must involve a wide range of stakeholder interests. Notably, it must extend beyond the profitability of individual investments or the desire to capture as much traffic as possible. China was able to address this requirement through its national planning framework—its five-year plans—which pull together the actions of its various ministries and other public bodies and provide an indication to private businesses of general policy directions.

Few countries have the planning procedures or centralized coordination and decision mechanisms that permitted China to achieve agreement among large networks of public and commercial actors, often having conflicting interests and the ability to act autonomously. However, there are other ways in which a more holistic approach to port planning can be developed in different contexts.

- The first is to expand the frontiers of traditional port planning to consider national economic and social objectives, the needs of the hinterland, the interests of the various supply chains that pass through the port, and the community within which each port is embedded.
- Consideration should also be given to the use of multistakeholder steering committees or a requirement for the plan to be jointly approved by relevant stakeholders or a higher-level organization that is able to take a wider overview, for example, the government's central planning unit.
- Finally, more opportunities can be created for public and private organizations to interact, encouraging each to look outside its silo when making decisions that will affect other groups. The opportunity to influence decisions should be a two-way street. For example, ports should have a say in the development of national rail infrastructure, and rail operators should be involved in the planning of rail yards within the ports.

networks, and the Belt and Road Initiative, which improved the connectivity of inland areas to seaports and established overland rail links to Europe.

The Port of Shanghai is a good example of this strategy. It played a vital role in the development of a comprehensive inland water transport network along the Yangtze River, the busiest river in the world in cargo volumes. The Port of Ningbo-Zhoushan, in contrast, has focused on developing sea-rail connections for its hinterland. Inland provinces, in their desire to export their manufactured products, also promoted the development of infrastructure that opened access to the coast.

The merger of separate ministries into a single Ministry of Transport (MoT) has improved coordination among freight transport modes, but China still lacks fully integrated multimodal freight transport policies, even though the 12th and 13th Five-Year Plans (spanning the years 2011 through 2020) advocated a comprehensive multimodal transport system, and the National Development and Reform Commission has also championed this idea.

A holistic approach is also apparent in the spatial planning of port cities, with logistics zones located well away from city centers, at points in the urban road networks where they cause minimum interference with other traffic. In some cases, administrative borders were modified to permit integrated development of ports and new manufacturing areas and to provide incentives for the relocation of established industries to suitable sites near the ports.

Holistic planning remains evident in current policies. The 14th Five-Year Plan (2021–25) focuses on achieving decarbonization and sustainable development (with comparatively less emphasis on international trade), meeting domestic demand, attracting higher value added industries, and stimulating innovation. These overall policy goals are translated to ports in several ways. China is promoting the merger of ports into regional groups to reduce the risk of overcapacity that stems partly from the shift of focus away from exports as drivers of economic growth. China's ambitious sustainability goals and emphasis on innovation and technological development steer port policies toward the digitalization of freight transport and the spread of terminal automation. Overseas investment by Chinese port companies is also well aligned with strategic policy goals set by the central government.

China began port decentralization in 1984 with pilot projects in Dalian and Tianjin designed to test the concept of joint port management. Lessons from the pilots led to a dual management system in which responsibilities were shared between the central and local governments. The MoT controlled strategic planning, port development, financing, and high-level regulation, while the local government was responsible for day-to-day management.

In the next step, the centrally funded port bureaus, which had hitherto held the dual roles of administrator and business operator, were split. Their administrative and regulatory functions were transferred to new port administrative authorities answering to provincial or municipal authorities. The bureaus' commercial functions were transferred to newly established state-owned port enterprises, which operated very much like private companies but under local government leadership, coordinated by central planning.

China's experience shows the risks of excessive decentralization, especially in preventing overcapacity. Equipped with financial resources to invest under the one-city, one-port strategy, many coastal cities invested in ports. This approach served the country well during the rapid expansion of exports but led to excess capacity when the economy shifted to consumption-led growth. Development of port clusters reflected recognition of the importance of combining decentralization with a mechanism for regional coordination.

Lesson 2: Consider how to balance decentralization, central coordination, and local initiative

Before 1978, China's port sector was very centralized. Port ownership and governance were under the control of the Ministry of Transport, which combined regulatory, administrative, and operational functions within a single entity. Local government had no control over port authorities, and all revenues from port operations accrued to the central government. Stepwise port reform led to the emergence of port companies operating on a commercial model, though still state owned. At the same time, more planning and development powers were transferred to municipal governments in the host cities, which were given the freedom to set their port development strategies within the framework of national plans. Decentralization empowered municipalities to develop their ports, bolstering local economies.

Today, most Chinese ports are local state-owned enterprises, which gives municipalities and provinces high-level control over port development policies, while ensuring that a commercially oriented corporate structure is responsible for day-to-day operations. China's state-owned port enterprises differ in three main ways from the autonomous port authorities that have become the norm in many western countries:

- They provide cargo handling services, either on their own or in joint ventures with private partners, rather than acting primarily as landlord ports, with port operations concessioned to private companies.
- Unlike port authorities in Spain, the United States, and elsewhere, they do not have regulatory responsibilities (for example, for the supervision of private port operators). Chinese port enterprises are regulated by local port administrative authorities.
- They are not required to make large dividend payments, so much of the cash flow from operations is available for reinvestment. Although they were originally funded by central or local government, the larger ports have been able to build up large equity reserves, making it easier for them to raise capital for new investments.

PORT-HINTERLAND CONNECTIVITY AND PORT CITIES

China's experiences in developing hinterland networks that contribute to the advancement of the interior include the following.

- A world-class inland waterway system was developed from almost nothing to handle 8 percent of Chinese freight (measured in ton-kilometers). Chinese seaports have invested in river ports that feed traffic to them, providing a logistics framework within which multiple companies can operate competing river shipping services.
- Coastal ports developed dry ports in cooperation with inland cities, thereby improving their connectivity to global trade. About 70 dry ports have been established in China, with minimal involvement of the central government. They encompass a wide range of ownership structures and business models, but only a few have rail connections. With regard to multimodalism, China still has a long way to go.
- In the container market segment, the share of rail is still below that in most advanced economies. Because of an extensive network of recently built toll roads, rail has trouble attracting container traffic, even over relatively long distances, and many of China's ports are still ill-equipped to handle rail traffic. Because the cargo volumes required to justify investments in infrastructure and

services are relatively large, some ports are likely to develop as rail hubs whereas others will not. The cases of Dalian and Ningbo-Zhoushan show that rail's share can be increased, and that developing rail can strengthen a port's competitive position. One of the lessons from China's experience is that multimodal connectivity should be promoted as soon as possible.

Lesson 3: Long-term competitiveness depends on strong networks and corridors linking ports with hinterlands

China's experience shows that long-term competitiveness depends on good multimodal connectivity with the hinterlands. In the early stages of port development, special economic zones (SEZs) were set up near gateway ports, which did not have and did not need connectivity with the interior via rail or inland waterways. However, as industrial activity shifted west, connectivity became vital. Since then, individual transport modes that had developed separately have been gradually aligned within a policy framework favoring multimodality.

China's experience illustrates the dangers of allowing export-oriented growth to become concentrated on the coast, resulting in large-scale internal migration, rapid urban growth, and disparities in income levels. It also provides a useful showcase for some of the policies that can be used to rebalance economic growth, including its Go West financial incentives and central government investments in urban infrastructure in selected inland cities and corridors.

Several large rivers in the world are not yet fulfilling their potential for environmentally friendly transport. Likewise, in many developing countries, the share of rail in container transport is limited. For these countries, China's experience is relevant. Even though it may seem like an uphill task to invest in rail and inland waterways, overreliance on road transport is unlikely to be sustainable in the long term.

One key policy choice in China was to link the development of hinterland transport networks to SEZs and inland container depots to support the formation of logistics and manufacturing clusters in the interior, with sustainable, reliable, and competitively priced transport services to ports. The policy of consolidating cargo flows at the point of origin rather than at the port is relevant for all developing economies aiming to use intermodal transport.

Lesson 4: Deploy land-use strategies to maximize the economic benefits of ports

Many of China's major ports have moved to new locations. In some cases, the new port areas were partly funded by redevelopment of the original city-center location for higher-value commercial and residential uses. Local governments have helped transform port cities based on long-term territorial development plans for the areas around new port sites. Investments in urban infrastructure for port-related industries and their workers have played a large role in this effort. As China's coastal cities have grown wealthier, these land-use strategies have balanced economic development objectives with growing demand for higher-quality residential areas.

The lesson offered by China's large urban agglomerations is that relocating port activities to areas with plenty of room for port, logistics, and manufacturing activities can facilitate city-center regeneration, particularly where land-use planning has been linked to land-based financing models.

This lesson is especially relevant for developing economies where port facilities are still located close to the urban center, often aggravating congestion and limiting opportunities to attract industrial and logistics activities.

Almost all of China's major ports have been moved to new locations within the past 20 to 30 years. In some cases, the new port areas have been partly funded by revenues from redevelopment of the older areas for higher-value uses. Some port cities have set up specially designed governance arrangements for the areas around new port sites and provided the supporting urban infrastructure for port-related industries and their workers.

Land-use and transportation planning units in China's port cities have often been proactive in facilitating the transfer of ports from congested city centers to more peripheral areas with deeper water and adjoining land for industrial development. Dalian and Shanghai clearly demonstrate the impact that port relocation can have on urban development, producing win-win scenarios that benefit both the city and the port.

HUMAN RESOURCES AND INNOVATION

Human capital underpins the development of any industry. Over the four decades covered by this report, the education of port employees was considered critical to developing the country. China expanded the role of universities and institutes to undertake the necessary research and produce graduates with the requisite professional expertise. In addition, vocational training centers sprang up in several provinces, providing a pipeline of competent artisans and making it possible to build the knowledge and skills of the workforce at every level within the organization.

BOX 3.5

Lesson 5: Invest in human capital and innovation as drivers of productivity and efficiency

The transition from government bureaucracies to commercially oriented port enterprises requires commercial capabilities and a performance culture. Manpower planning in port enterprises created a culture of responsibility and accountability, whereas in many countries port work is still regarded as either unskilled and low paid or a comfortable job for life. The massive technological change that is already taking place, and will continue for the foreseeable future, will make port workers an increasingly valuable resource, requiring continuing investment in training and career development. This is an important lesson for other countries.

The three main tools used for developing human resources in Chinese ports—specialist training, performance-related pay, and good channels of communication—do not cost a lot of money but may require a change of mindset. A good starting point would be an increase in the status of human-resource managers,

a formal strategy for human-resource development, and personalized career-development programs.

The use of information and communication technology in ports is another area in which China is developing a significant advantage, in part because of its well-educated younger workers. New technology is producing large efficiency gains by coordinating the actions of multiple players in port supply chains and allowing each individual to do more. These productivity improvements will be of increasing importance in countries that—like China—have aging populations.

Although internationally available software was used during the early stages of port development, Chinese ports have now mostly developed their own. The main challenge is to commit supply chain partners to digital platforms and services. For instance, customs authorities play a large role in so-called port community systems.

These skills have required continuous adaptation as port technology has progressed. As with the container revolution in the late 1960s, digitalization will produce great changes in logistics, with major implications for human capital. In the past decade the focus on research into digitalization by dedicated teams has produced a continuing stream of innovations, leading to new business models and technologies that improve efficiency and sustainability.

Some of those innovations have been centrally funded, such as the intelligent shipping program; others have come from port enterprises (Ministry of Transport et al. 2019). For example, China Merchants Port Holdings invests heavily in testing emerging technologies, and Qingdao Port has signed cooperation agreements with several public and private institutions to improve information and communication technology and digital maturity throughout the port cluster.

The 12th Five-Year Plan (2011–15) called for a "comprehensive, smart, green, and safe transportation system." That goal was translated into the use of multimodal transport systems, greening practices, and digital solutions to enhance sustainability in the port sector. The use of onshore power when vessels are berthed and electric gantry cranes in the container stacks are good examples of the green use of current infrastructure. About 5,200 terminals have been equipped with shore power capabilities, and 2,300 rubber-tired container gantry cranes have been switched to electricity.

PORT GOVERNANCE AND FINANCE

China's port development combines commercialization with the economic, social, and environmental policy goals of the central government. Although policies initially prioritized economic development and internationalization, they were later expanded to include innovation, environmental sustainability, reductions in the negative externalities of port activities for host cities, and narrower socioeconomic disparities between coastal and inland regions. Various initiatives were launched to reduce emissions from port operations and ships in port. The environmental efficiency of Chinese ports increased as a result, but the potential for further improvement is great.

In China, the state-owned enterprise (SOE) model ensured that the central government retained just enough control over port development. Although many private foreign companies act as service providers, the port enterprises are SOEs and, consistent with China's overall institutional structure, follow the broad direction set out in national five-year plans. For instance, the SOEs increasingly invest in innovation and technology and have developed ambitious environmental initiatives, in line with the current five-year plan. Some countries may find China's governance context inapplicable but may still learn useful lessons despite the differences.

State ownership of port enterprises in China has ensured that the actions and investments of those enterprises supported development strategies within and beyond the port gate, and that they were consistent with broad macroeconomic and social policies. Such coordination is not necessarily dependent on who owns and operates port assets, but, in a relatively weak legal and contractual environment, coordination within the state sector was arguably easier than it would have been under a public-private partnership approach. Port SOEs have also

BOX 3.6

Lesson 6: Government plays a role in creating the right environment for port financing while balancing economic, social, and environmental objectives

State-owned enterprises (SOEs) have combined an increasingly commercial approach to port development with a simultaneous focus on socioeconomic development, within a framework of strong central planning. This model has supported rapid port development while simultaneously addressing other policy goals, such as urban redevelopment, economic integration of the hinterlands, and prevention of overcapacity. Initially, the SOEs helped upgrade the commercial and technological capabilities of ports through joint ventures; later, they played an important role in integrating the hinterland and coastal economies through investments in dry ports. The SOE model also enabled China to address overcapacity by establishing regional port clusters, an outcome that would be extremely challenging in a private sector–led model of port development.

The commercialization of seaports has been one of the main features of port policy worldwide over the past 40 years and has led to large efficiency gains and improvements in performance. In China, the commercial orientation of SOEs has been guided by a mixture of clear policy objectives, performance incentives, and central planning. The decentralized partnership model may also have helped improve SOE governance.

However, commercialization may have overstepped the mark in several instances, putting financial performance ahead of the economic, social, and environmental concerns of the local or regional community. In addition, experience with SOEs has not been as positive in other countries, where a landlord port model may be more appropriate in some contexts.

There are other ways to combine financial and social objectives, in addition to the system of local SOEs developed in China, including the following:

- Municipal ownership of ports or a direct local government role in overall port planning
- Broadening the board of directors of autonomous ports to widen stakeholder representation, which should include levels of government responsible for transportation and logistics functions
- Regulation of port development through approvals and permits to ensure appropriate mitigation or compensation for adverse consequences
- Closer monitoring and supervision of port operations by independent bodies, with higher reporting standards and wider dissemination of results
- More involvement of port managers in economic development initiatives and planning for land use and transportation
- Empowerment of local communities through engagement with nongovernmental organizations and by tying port development to community benefits agreements that recognize and address externalities and support local economic opportunities.

Although priorities can be balanced in different ways, the Chinese experience offers important lessons for ports around the world. However, that experience may not be easily replicable. Few other countries can use competition between local government SOEs to promote good performance as readily as China can. In many countries, governance weaknesses within the public sector have turned SOEs into rent-seeking monopolies, with a high risk of underperformance.

benefited from implicit government guarantees when seeking financing, enabling them to fund their rapid expansion at relatively low cost. At the same time, strong human-resource and management practices have ensured that port SOEs remained performance oriented and were provided incentives to adopt new technologies and business practices.

China's experience shows that it is possible to assemble a diverse set of funding options for port development. After initial reliance on state funding, funding sources were diversified. Foreign investment was promoted via joint ventures,

Lesson 7: Broaden access to the finance and public support needed to develop a competitive port ecosystem

China's initial port reforms gave local governments the incentive to develop their ports. In addition to delegating regulatory and operational responsibilities to the local level, the Ministry of Transport also allowed a portion of port profits to be reinvested. The subsequent clear separation between regulatory and operational functions allowed port state-owned enterprises to focus on maximizing efficiency and to adjust pricing and service offerings. Local governments diversified sources of funding for port development early on by forming joint ventures to attract foreign direct investment, which also brought in new technology and modern management practices. State funding was provided for port development, but the importance of direct state funding diminished over time and was replaced by commercial financing sources. State support shifted to ensuring connectivity with the hinterland, improving environmental performance, and transforming the port-city ecosystem. Tax incentives for the relocation of industries to new port areas also enhanced their economic attractiveness.

Many emerging economies still have relatively weak banking systems and poorly developed stock exchanges, and local investors may be reluctant to finance ports because of strict and sometimes uncertain regulatory regimes. Experience from China shows that it is possible to move from a regime in which port developments are financed wholly from the central government budget to one in which ports have access to a wide range of financial instruments with different maturities, collateral requirements,

and risk-reward ratios. Opportunities beyond traditional finance (government grants and bank loans) are therefore worth investigating. The net should be cast wide, going beyond national boundaries to tap into international expertise and financing.

In the past, many countries have used the landlord port-concession system to attract capital and management expertise in the same transaction. This is still a popular, well-tested model. But Chinese experience has shown that it is possible—and in some cases may be desirable—to decouple the two, allowing ports in other countries to access often-cheaper capital from investors that do not necessarily want to become involved in port management.

This leaves open the question of where the necessary management expertise will come from. One option is joint ventures to which the overseas partners contribute management skills rather than financial resources. In the past this expertise has usually been acquired through short-term management contracts, but such arrangements have proved to be unattractive to the most desirable partners because of their short duration and low returns. A longer and more rewarding arrangement, such as a joint venture, might prove more attractive and—as China has shown—would satisfy the need for continuous upgrades of port operations.

Another option would be for international aid packages to include the transfer of know-how and management skills through joint ventures or long-term mentorship arrangements paid for by the donor countries.

which attracted not only finance, but also knowledge, skills, and equipment for port management and operations. Foreign aid also increased, with the World Bank being an important partner. Its first transport loan to China was to support the ports of Guangzhou, Shanghai, and Tianjin.

Recognizing that local governments needed incentives to invest and improve the operational efficiency of the ports in their jurisdictions, the MoT altered its financing arrangements to allow a portion of port profits to be used by the local port authority for improvements. Success of the port also meant more profits for the local port authority to use for further improvements, thus creating a virtuous circle.

Ensuring that local government had incentives to support port development was a critical step in the evolution of policy. It widened access to finance by contributing to the development of financing companies set up by local governments. It made possible awards of tax relief and subsidies to ports. And it encouraged the building of supporting facilities such as land-transport infrastructure. Inland provinces could invest in transportation systems through partnerships with coastal ports, which helped to grow China's ports and in turn revitalized inland industries, boosting China's economy.

China's experience also shows that funding sources can be diversified over time. In addition, the share of state funding can be reduced, and the share of commercial funding increased. China has also demonstrated that profitable port companies can finance a substantial part of their own investment needs. Good operating results allow port companies to reinvest their available cash flow (earnings before interest, taxes, depreciation, and amortization [EBITDA]) as well as attract more equity through foreign direct investment, domestic private equity partners, or stock offerings.

In the early stages of port-linked economic development, high levels of uncertainty about demand will make state support and investment necessary, including for connected infrastructure. In the early period of China's opening, capacity shortages in ports were overcome through large, sustained investments from the central government. Without these investments, bottlenecks would have emerged as a constraint to growth.

That early investments were funded chiefly by the central government is partly explained by the institutional context, but also by the relatively high uncertainty about demand. However, state support for port development was not limited to the initial phase of economic opening. In the decades since, port development has been supported by all levels of government in China. The central government has given port cities SEZ status, provided state funding for port infrastructure, invested in hinterland infrastructure, improved the quality of customs procedures by enabling the development of dry ports and bonded zones, and invested in innovation and education. Regional and local governments have developed attractive tax schemes for port development, invested in hinterland infrastructure, and provided incentives for the relocation of industries to new port areas. State-owned banks have provided funding to port enterprises.

BOX 3.8

Lesson 8: Test the waters before scaling up

Chinese port reforms have not been devoid of false starts, but there has been a willingness to change course when individual policy changes have failed to produce the desired results. Pilot projects have played an important role in developing Chinese thinking, and the authorities have encouraged the replication of successful innovations elsewhere, particularly in port finance.

However, there is a need for leadership, both to drive the reform process and to monitor and evaluate the results. Although the most visible initiatives appear to have occurred at the local level, deeper probing suggests that softer interventions by the central government have been the main guiding force. China adopted an unusually holistic approach to export-led economic development in which the central government is the only body with the authority to coordinate the many other players involved.

Beginning with the opening of the Chinese economy in 1978, the port sector followed an incremental approach to policy making. Understanding that each port faces unique circumstances, the central government embarked on a gradual program of decentralization that transferred powers to local authorities, with the first step being targeted pilot projects.

Although decision-making power remained ultimately in the hands of the central government, local authorities were better placed to understand the needs of their own ports and better able to optimize resources and devise incentives for ports to improve performance. This relationship and division of responsibility between the central and regional governments was evident when ports were being aligned with central government guidelines, which identified port development as a top priority in the Port Law of 2004 and successive five-year plans dating from 1991. In a context in which international trade was booming, the central government coupled governance reforms with other elements, notably financial reforms, expansion of hinterland transport systems, workforce improvements, and digitalization.

The transition over the past three decades from an export-oriented economy to one driven by domestic consumption reflected another mind shift in government. The overcapacity of certain ports that resulted from early decentralization was remedied through the formation of integrated groups of ports. And the coordinated development of other modes of transport—such as inland water transport along the Yangtze River—was designed to accommodate new flow patterns. Transport-related ministerial functions were merged into a single Ministry of Transport tasked with improving coordination among the different modes. Connectivity of digital systems has also been strongly encouraged, reducing administrative burdens and facilitating cross-border trade through the development of a single-window system. Finally, the Belt and Road Initiative has given China a role in the development of a global ports network.

China's port reforms since 1978 have followed a gradual experimental process characterized by ample piloting before scaling up. Decentralization of port governance began with an initial trial at the Port of Tianjin in 1984; only after the trial was deemed a success did other ports follow.

Likewise, the central government soon realized that more financing from a variety of sources was needed to achieve sector development goals. Financing policies were reformed over decades as China experimented with foreign direct investment, port charges, and greater autonomy for local port authorities and port enterprises. Reforms to the development of human capital, with new financial incentives for workers and upgrades in education and training, also resulted in greater efficiency.

The advantage of this gradual reform process is that China was able to experiment with and correct processes that did not work for its ports industry. The long timeline may also reflect China's deliberate, conservative approach to policy during this period. However, a similarly drawn-out timeline may not suit other countries seeking more rapid development (Humphreys et al. 2019). At the same time, looking at the recent clustering of coastal ports, an important lesson from China is to take a cautious view about developing ports as isolated elements, and to always take developments in neighboring areas into consideration.

REFERENCES

Humphreys, Martin, Aiga Stokenberga, Matias Herrera Dappe, Atsushi Iimi, and Olivier Hartmann. 2019. *Port Development and Competition in East and Southern Africa: Prospects and Challenges*. International Development in Focus. Washington, DC: World Bank. https://openknowledge.worldbank.org/handle/10986/31897.

Ministry of Transport, Cyberspace Administration of China, National Development and Reform Commission, Ministry of Education, Ministry of Science and Technology, Ministry of Industry and Information Technology, and Ministry of Finance. 2019. Notice of "Intelligent Shipping Development Guidance." 关于印发《智能航运发展指导意见》的通知 (in Chinese). Beijing. https://xxgk.mot.gov.cn/jigou/haishi/201911/P020191119606591225864.pdf.

Policies Affecting Multimodal Transport in China, 2011–19

TABLE A.1 Policies concerning multimodal transport in China, 2011–19

ISSUE DATE	POLICY DOCUMENT	ISSUING ENTITY	IMPLICATIONS FOR MULTIMODAL TRANSPORT
November 2011	Agreement on partnership in railway-waterway multimodal transport	MoT and, formerly, MoR[a]	The two ministries were to coordinate more closely on (1) improving plans for developing railway-waterway multimodal transport, (2) facilitating the building of infrastructure, (3) improving supporting policies and standards, (4) improving transportation organization, (5) sharing information, and (6) fostering leading enterprises.
June 2013	Guiding opinions on the transportation sector, advancing healthy development of the logistics industry	MoT	Multimodal transport was to be considered the principal focus when using transportation to promote the logistics industry.
October 2014	Mid- and long-term plan for developing the logistics industry (2014–20)	State Council	Multimodal transport was prioritized in 12 major projects. Development of multiple transportation modes was encouraged, including railway-maritime, railway-waterway, highway-railway, and land-air.
July 2015	Notification about conducting multimodal transport demonstration projects	MoT, NDRC	Demonstration projects were to be implemented for equipment and technologies designed for rapid transshipment, and for innovations in the organization of multimodal transport.
June 2016	Implementation plan for building a sound market environment and advancing the fusion of transportation and logistics	NDRC	The goal was to promote multimodal transport and expand international multimodal transport services.
July 2016	The 13th Five-Year Plan for the development of a comprehensive transportation service	MoT	The target for growth in container multimodal transport was set at an annual rate of 10 percent. A draft law to enhance the overarching design of multimodal transport was produced. Plans for multimodal transport corridors and improved infrastructure were commissioned.
October 2016	Plan for developing China-Europe cargo trains (2016–20)	Office of the Steering Panel for Pushing forward the Belt and Road Initiative	The plan proposed to optimize the system of organizing transportation, collection, and distribution of freight, thus improving the efficiency and benefits of China-Europe cargo trains.

continued

TABLE A.1, *continued*

ISSUE DATE	POLICY DOCUMENT	ISSUING ENTITY	IMPLICATIONS FOR MULTIMODAL TRANSPORT
December 2016	Action plan for promoting the building of logistics channels (2016–20)	MoT, NDRC	Multimodal transport was to be facilitated by logistics. Outlined the development of multimodal transport systems for containers, semitrailers, and bulk commodities.
January 2017	Notice on encouraging the development of multimodal transport	MoT and 18 other departments	Promoted the development of an efficient and smooth multimodal transport system through creation of an enabling market environment, deeper reforms, greater information sharing, and enhanced cooperation with foreign countries. A target was set to increase the volume of multimodal freight in 2020 to 1.5 times that of 2015.
February 2017	The 13th Five-Year Plan for developing a modern comprehensive transportation system	State Council	Aimed to develop multimodal transport of bulk commodities and specialty goods; set improved and uniform rules for multimodal transport and systems for operators; implemented a "single document" multimodal transport service model; and accelerated the development of technical standards for special equipment and apparatus for railway multimodal transport.
May 2017	The 13th Five-Year Plan for developing railway container multimodal transport	NDRC, MoT, China Railway	Set goals that included facilitating the development of railway container multimodal transport and building an integrated, networked, standardized, and information technology–based container multimodal transport system.
September 2018	Three-year action plan for promoting transport structural adjustment (2018–20)	State Council	Set key goals for 2020, including to (1) increase railway and waterway transport volumes by 30 percent (1.1 trillion tons) and 7.5 percent (500 trillion tons), respectively, compared with 2017; (2) cut roads' share of bulk cargo by 440 billion tons; (3) expand multimodal transportation volumes by 20 percent annually; (4) enhance ports' rail connections by continuing to construct railway container yards; (5) boost direct transport from river to sea; (6) continue construction of multimodal demonstration projects and operational monitoring of these projects, as well as innovations in transportation organization; and (7) reserve land for special railway lines and waterfronts for wharves for rail-water transshipment.
September 2019	Outline for building China's strength in transport	State Council	Proposed (1) shifting away from relatively independent development of transportation models toward their integrated development, (2) building national and regional multimodal transport hubs, (3) improving service quality of transshipment and hinterland transportation, and (4) creating a green and efficient modern logistics system based on intermodal transport and the integration of transport infrastructure.

Source: Xiao and Liu (2018), supplemented by research for this volume.
Note: MoR = Ministry of Railways; MoT = Ministry of Transport; NDRC = National Development and Reform Commission.
a. The Ministry of Railways was merged with the Ministry of Transport in 2013.

REFERENCE

Xiao, J. H., and X. Liu. 2018. "Development of Multimodal Transport in China." In *Contemporary Logistics in China*, edited by Bing-lian Liu, Shao-ju Lee, Ling Wang, Xiang Li, and Jian-hua Xiao, 137–60. Singapore: Springer.

Complete List of China's Dry Ports

TABLE B.1 **Profile of China's dry ports**

DRY PORT	PROFILE					SERVICES			
	OWNERSHIP	CONNECTED COASTAL PORT	YEAR ESTABLISHED	CAPACITY (TEU/YEAR)	AREA (HECTARES)	CLEARANCE	STORAGE	FREIGHT FORWARDING	OTHER
Yiwu	Ningbo port and local company	Ningbo	2002	1,000,000	1,601	✓	✓	✓	Goods collection, deconsolidation
Shenyang	Dalian and Yingkou ports	Dalian and Yingkou	2003	150,000	200	✓	✓	✓	Goods collection, transshipment
Nanchang	Local company	Multiple	2006	—	—	✓	✓		—
Shijiazhuang	Tianjin port and local company	Tianjin	2006	205,000	255	✓	✓		—
Baotou	Tianjin port and local company	Tianjin	2007	38,000	190	✓	✓		—
Manzhouli	Railway company and Qinhuangdao port	Qinhuangdao	2007	250,000	180	✓	✓		—
Sanming	Xiamen port and local company	Xiamen	2007	50,000	30	✓	✓		—
Linyi	Railway company and local company	Rizhao	2008	120,000	180	✓	✓		—
Shaoguan	Yantian port and local company	Yantian	2008	100,000	100	✓	✓		Bonded area, logistics
Houma	Tianjin port and local company	Tianjin and Qingdao	2009	60,000	149	✓	✓		—
Quzhou	Ningbo port and local company	Ningbo	2009	50,000	54	✓	✓		—
Urumqi	Tianjin port and railway company	Tianjin	2009	—	—	✓	✓		—
Beijing Pinggu	Tianjin port and local company	Tianjin	2010	200,000	200	✓	✓		Bonded area, deconsolidation
Chengdu	Local company and railway company	Multiple	2010	2,500,000	2,140	✓	✓	✓	Manufacturing, deconsolidation
Handan	Tianjin port and local company	Tianjin	2010	—	—	✓	✓		—
Harbin	Railway company	Dalian	2010	100,000	350	✓	✓	✓	Goods collection, transshipment
Kunming	Local company and railway company	Multiple	2010	500,000	1,300	✓	✓	✓	—
Longyan	Xiamen port and local company	Xiamen	2010	90,000	86	✓	✓		Deconsolidation
Nanning	Local company	Beibu Gulf	2010	—	53–55	✓	✓		—
Xi'an	Local government	Multiple	2010	—	4,460	✓	✓		Bonded area, transshipment
Changsha	Local company	Multiple	2011	—	—	✓	✓		—

continued

TABLE B.1, *continued*

| DRY PORT | PROFILE | | | | | SERVICES | | | |
	OWNERSHIP	CONNECTED COASTAL PORT	YEAR ESTABLISHED	CAPACITY (TEU/YEAR)	AREA (HECTARES)	CLEARANCE	STORAGE	FREIGHT FORWARDING	OTHER
Mudanjiang	Local company and Dalian port	Dalian	2011	200,000	270	√	√		—
Zhangjiakou	Tianjin port and local enterprise	Tianjin	2011	100,000	300	√	√		—
Zhengzhou	Local company and railway company	Multiple	2011	600,000	1,630	√	√		Goods collection, deconsolidation
Lanzhou	Local government	Multiple	2016	300,000	1,200	√	√	√	Manufacturing, deconsolidation
Anyang	Local company and Rizhao port	Rizhao	—	200,000	800	√	√	√	—
Xining	Tianjin port and railway company	Tianjin and Rizhao	—	100,00	145	√	√	√	—

Source: China Waterborne Transport Research Institute (WTI).
Note: — = not available; TEU = twenty-foot equivalent unit.

CPSIA information can be obtained
at www.ICGtesting.com
Printed in the USA
BVHW020617120123
656153BV00022B/202

9 781464 818493